THE SHAKER CHAIR
CHARLES R. MULLER   TIMOTHY D. RIEMAN

THE SHAKER CHAIR
CHARLES R. MULLER   TIMOTHY D. RIEMAN

FOREWORD
JERRY GRANT

ILLUSTRATIONS
STEPHEN METZGER

PHOTOGRAPHY
TIMOTHY D. RIEMAN

DESIGN AND LAYOUT
STEPHEN METZGER
TIMOTHY D. RIEMAN

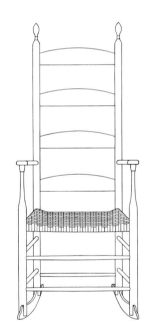

The University of Massachusetts Press

AMHERST

Originally published in 1984 by The Canal Press
First paperback edition, 1992, by The University of Massachusetts Press
All rights reserved
Copyright © 1984 by Charles R. Muller and Timothy D. Rieman
Illustrations © 1984 by Stephen Metzger
Printed in the United States of America

LC 91–40646
ISBN 0–87023–795–0

Library of Congress Cataloging-in-Publication Data
Muller, Charles R.
The Shaker chair / Charles R. Muller, Timothy D. Rieman ;
foreword, Jerry Grant ; illustrations, Stephen Metzger ;
photography, Timothy D. Rieman. — 1st pbk. ed.
          p.   cm.
Originally published: Canal Winchester, Ohio : Canal Press, 1984.
Includes bibliographical references and index.
ISBN 0–87023–795–0 (pbk. : alk. paper)
1. Chairs, Shaker. 2. Chairs—United States—History—19th century.
          I. Rieman, Timothy D.   II. Title
          [NK2713.M84 1992]   91–40646
          749' .32'088288—dc20

British Library Cataloguing in Publication data are available.

Frontispiece: Armed Rocker, ca. 1840 *(The Sherman Collection)*

CONTENTS

FOREWORD

Thousands did stop by the New Lebanon chair shop or bought chairs through its mail order catalogues. The century and a half long popularity of Shaker chairs reflects the strength of the design and the quality of the workmanship. *We want a good plain substantial article,* Brother Orren Haskins advised young Shakers, *yea, one that bears credit to our profession and tells who and what we are, true and honest before all the world, without hypocrisy or any faults covering. The world at large can Scarcely keep pace with it self in its stiles and fassions which last out a short time, when something still more worthless or absurd takes its place, let good enough alone.*

The Shakers did develop a good plain substantial article in the chairs they made for sale as well as the thousands made for their own use in work and worship. To encourage the feeling of union between and within their communities, the Shakers demanded uniformity in their manufactures. The chairs that resulted from such regulation are strikingly similar but, from century to century, community to community and craftsman to craftsman, variations appear.

Timothy Rieman and Charles Muller have studied both the uniformity and variety in the Shakers' chairs. The combined approach of examining the historic records and then, from the perspective of the craft of chairmaking, examining the chairs themselves to discover the hidden records they contain adds significant insight into our knowledge of the Shaker chair.

At a time when Shaker chairs—originals, imitations and reproductions—are changing hands nearly as frequently as they did at the peak of the Shakers' manufacturing, *The Shaker Chair* is a welcome and valuable resource for the novice as well as the senior-most student of Shaker furniture.

Jerry V. Grant
Hancock, Massachusetts
1984

PREFACE

As the two of us journeyed one October afternoon to visit the Stickley Furniture Company in Fayetteville, New York, in search of the correct identity of what had for years been called a Hancock Shaker chair, we committed ourselves to author a book on Shaker chairs. It seemed a natural combination: Tim with his eye for design and skill as a chairmaker and Chuck with his talent as a writer; Tim with his interest and residence in New Lebanon and Chuck with his attention centered in Union Village; both with years of experience in the world of antiques in general and Shaker in particular; and both with a spirit of inquiry and learning.

What started out to be a handy guide to Shaker chairs slowly evolved into a major project as we began reading the journals and account books and discovered examples that reflected changes in the development of this common household object. We soon became impressed with the research done by Edward D. and Faith Andrews almost half a century ago. We were able to take advantage of their pioneering research. We read the original documents that they consulted, as well as material that has come to light since then. We read and studied manuscripts at museums and libraries from the Hancock Shaker Village to the Library of Congress.

We visited many places we had previously been but now with a specific goal and new insight. We made new friends and visited collections few others had seen. We traveled together—often with a typewriter set up in the back of a van. We studied apart.

This book is the result of our joint efforts, two people seeking to understand the subject matter for themselves. In the process we enlisted the assistance of Stephen Metzger to show graphically what we were learning.

In this book, the attribution of chairs as Shaker and the association of a chair with a particular community is based on consideration of oral tradition, provenance, place of discovery, visual examination, evaluation of design features, historic photographs, and information found in written resources. While we have read the publications of other authors and the primary sources cited

therein, we also found material regarding chairs that has not been previously noted. This additional information, and a careful analysis of the chairs, has enabled us to draw different conclusions than other authors.

We started this book with some preconceptions which were confirmed in our research while others did not hold up to intense scrutiny and led us to new insight. One example was our assumption that the community of Hancock made chairs. This Shaker village had a number of notable cabinetmakers and various chairs associated with it. But the primary material does not substantiate that the cabinetmakers at Hancock made chairs. We discovered information external to the world of the Shakers that documents some formerly "Hancock" chairs as having been manufactured in the world. Examination and evaluation of other "Hancock" chairs show style features like those of nearby New Lebanon. Journal references confirm the purchase of chairs from that community by Hancock. Thus, the assumption that there was chairmaking at Hancock did not withstand close examination. The same process occurred numerous times in shaping our understanding of the Shaker chair.

In using this book to determine the community origin of a particular chair, the reader should consider all elements of the chair. A comparison of pommels *and* back slats *and* arm style *and* rocker shape . . . a look at the *total* chair . . . is necessary. The workmanship of some communities is similar and, therefore, often difficult to differentiate. This is particularly true of the early chairs.

Quotations from original sources are set in italics. The misspellings are not typographical errors but the reproduction of the spelling found in the manuscripts. This adherence to the original writings enhances the reader's historical perspective. In some instances photographs of the handwritten text are used, as typesetting loses the personal flavor of the journals and letters. We have chosen to use the terminology of the Shakers when possible, i.e. pommel instead of the contemporary term finial; bar instead of shawl or cushion rail.

Included in this book are photographs of some chairs that have been repaired or restored. These are often used without comment because the restorations are in keeping with the original design.

The Shaker Chair is an attempt to delineate what the Shaker chair is and, in some cases, what it is not. Many chairs which have previously been called "Shaker" do not appear in this volume because of our conviction that they were not made by the United Society of Believers. Others do not appear because of their uncertain origins. Perhaps some future scholars will be able to more adequately ascertain the proper origins for these chairs. We realize that this book is not a final statement but a contribution to the resource material available for further study.

CHARLES R. MULLER
TIMOTHY D. RIEMAN

ACKNOWLEDGEMENTS

While preparing *The Shaker Chair* has been intense for the authors and the illustrator, many people have helped in the production of this volume and deserve recognition and the expression of our gratitude.

Acknowledgements must begin with Brenda Muller, Molly Backup, and Julie Metzger. They, as well as the other members of our families, have given time, energy, and interest. They have participated in the research, reading, typing, editing, and criticism of this book. We express a special "thank you" for their great patience and support.

From the beginning, Jerry Grant, friend, oval box maker, scholar, and now the director of Hancock Shaker Village, Inc., has been a source of encouragement, direction and information. He was our obvious choice to write the "Foreword."

We wish to acknowledge the pioneering work of Edward D. and Faith Andrews as a stimulus and a model for our efforts. The material included in the *Community Industries* has remained for fifty years the most accurate and comprehensive study on Shaker chairs.

Extensive research of original Shaker manuscripts has been an important part of this study. The authors were assisted in this by Katharine Booth, Wendell and Vi Hess, Nancy Hillenberg, and Diana Van Kolken. Additional sources were the following individuals and their corresponding libraries: Howard Fertig, Julia Neal, and Brother Thomas Whitaker; Katheryn Carrel, Ohio Historical Society, Columbus, Ohio; Gayle Chandler and Beatrice K. Taylor, Henry Francis du Pont Winterthur Museum, Winterthur, Delaware; Jan Clower, Bexley Public Library, Bexley, Ohio; Mrs. Jean Crispen, Fruitlands Museums, Harvard, Massachusetts; Elaine M. Harrison, Kentucky Library, Western Kentucky University, Bowling Green, Kentucky; James Holmberg, The Filson Club, Louisville, Kentucky; Brothers Theodore E. Johnson and Arnold Hadd, United Society of Shakers at Sabbathday Lake, Maine; Ann Kelley and Maria Larson, The Shaker Museum, Old Chatham, New York; Sarah A. Kinter and Charles F. Thompson, Canterbury Shaker Village, Inc., East Canterbury, New Hampshire; Robert F.W. Meader, Hancock Shaker Community, Inc., Pittsfield,

Massachusetts; and Kermit Pike and Charles Sherrill, Western Reserve Historical Society, Cleveland, Ohio.

We examined chairs in museums and private homes; people were gracious and hospitable. Deep appreciation goes to the following individuals for opening their doors to the authors: Robert and Katharine Booth, Mr. and Mrs. Kenneth E. Brooker, Mr. and Mrs. John P. Carr, Frank J. Cutadean, Joe Degorgis and Joy Van Alystene, Charles Flint, Natalie and Marvin Gliedman, Douglas and Cornelia Hamel, Hazel and Leslie Hamilton, Robert Hamilton, Mr. and Mrs. Richard Helir, Jane Murphy, Gus and June Nelson, Tom and Janet Pavlovic, Richard and Betty Ann Rasso, Jack and Betty Rhodus, John Keith Russell, Milton and Joan Sherman, Joanne Sprowls, James and Winola Stokes. Appreciation also goes to the following persons and their corresponding institutions: Charles A. Weyerhaeuser, The Art Complex at Duxbury, Massachusetts; Richard Kathman, Canterbury Shaker Village, Inc.; Don Adams and Kenneth Wilson, Edison Institute, Henry Ford Museum and Greenfield, Village, Dearborn, Michigan; Richard S. Reed, Fruitlands Museums; Jack Reynolds, Golden Lamb Inn, Lebanon, Ohio; John H. Ott, former director of Hancock Shaker Village, Inc.; Mercer County Historical Society, Harrodsburg, Kentucky; John Scherer and Peter Shaver, New York State Museum, Albany, New York; Patricia and Peter Laskovski and Viki Sand, The Shaker Museum; Ed Nickels and James C. Thomas, Shakertown at Pleasant Hill, Harrodsburg, Kentucky; John Campbell, Shakertown at South Union, South Union, Kentucky; Sisters R. Mildred Barker and Francis A. Carr, United Society of Shakers at Sabbathday Lake; Vicki Visintainer, Warren County Historical Society, Lebanon, Ohio; and Jairus B. Barnes, The Western Reserve Historical Society.

Throughout the study, writing and editing of *The Shaker Chair*, people have been extremely helpful in giving of knowledge and special skills, especially Roger Billings, Judy Grant, John Kassay, E. Ray Pearson, Virginia Rowe, June Sprigg, Robert and Mary Lou Sutter and Herbert Wisbey. Sandy McNay processed and printed the photographs in the book. Photographs from the collection of John Keith Russell were taken by David Smith.

While many people have assisted during the past few years in the preparation of this book, there are those whose labors extend back over two centuries. The Shakers with their idealistic concepts and world view developed a distinctive style of household furnishings. *The Shaker Chair* is a tribute to these spiritually courageous people.

"(A) the Shakers didn't work from kits, and
(B) they were religiously motivated."

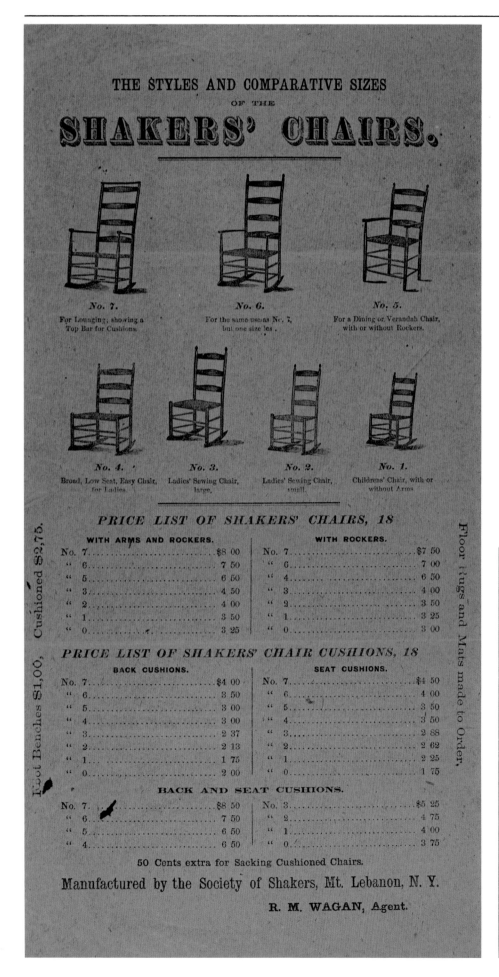

THE STYLES AND COMPARATIVE SIZES OF THE
SHAKERS' CHAIRS.

No. 7.
For Lounging; showing a Top Bar for Cushions.

No. 6.
For the same uses as No. 7, but one size less.

No. 5.
For a Dining or Verandah Chair, with or without Rockers.

No. 4.
Broad, Low Seat, Easy Chair, for Ladies.

No. 3.
Ladies' Sewing Chair, large.

No. 2.
Ladies' Sewing Chair, small.

No. 1.
Childrens' Chair, with or without Arms.

PRICE LIST OF SHAKERS' CHAIRS, 18

WITH ARMS AND ROCKERS.		WITH ROCKERS.	
No. 7	$8 00	No. 7	$7 50
" 6	7 50	" 6	7 00
" 5	6 50	" 4	6 50
" 3	4 50	" 3	4 00
" 2	4 00	" 2	3 50
" 1	3 50	" 1	3 25
" 0	3 25	" 0	3 00

PRICE LIST OF SHAKERS' CHAIR CUSHIONS, 18

BACK CUSHIONS.		SEAT CUSHIONS.	
No. 7	$4 00	No. 7	$4 50
" 6	3 50	" 6	4 00
" 5	3 00	" 5	3 50
" 4	3 00	" 4	3 50
" 3	2 37	" 3	2 88
" 2	2 13	" 2	2 62
" 1	1 75	" 1	2 25
" 0	2 00	" 0	1 75

BACK AND SEAT CUSHIONS.

No. 7	$8 50	No. 3	$5 25
" 6	7 50	" 2	4 75
" 5	6 50	" 1	4 00
" 4	6 50	" 0	3 75

50 Cents extra for Sacking Cushioned Chairs.

Manufactured by the Society of Shakers, Mt. Lebanon, N. Y.

R. M. WAGAN, Agent.

Floor Rugs and Mats made to Order.

Foot Benches $1,00, Cushioned $2,75.

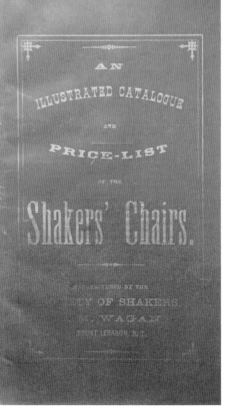

AN ILLUSTRATED CATALOGUE AND PRICE-LIST OF THE Shakers' Chairs.

MANUFACTURED BY THE SOCIETY OF SHAKERS. R. M. WAGAN MOUNT LEBANON, N. Y.

Paper label, ca.1870. New Lebanon, New York. The only known label of this style. (Courtesy of Hancock Shaker Village, Inc., Pittsfield, Massachusetts)

Armed rocker, 1873. New Lebanon, New York. Number 6. Original red cushion with black border. Attached to cushion bar and posts with the strings. (Courtesy of The Shaker Museum, Old Chatham, New York)

Page inserted in chair catalogue, 1874. The only color page in the catalogue. Illustrates the color of the upholstered chairs, foot stools and rugs. (Courtesy of the Fruitlands Museums, Harvard, Massachusetts)

Armed rocker, ca.1850. New Lebanon, New York. Finely detailed side scroll arm. Rocker blade similar to those used on the earliest production chairs. Birdseye maple. Dark varnish finish. (The Sherman Collection)

Armed rocker, ca.1820. Enfield, Connecticut. Tall slender proportions. Boldly graduated back slats. Curly maple. Varnish finish. (Courtesy of Hancock Shaker Village, Inc., Pittsfield, Massachusetts)

Armless rocker, ca. 1840. Canterbury, New Hampshire. Large back slats, short rockers. Varnish finish. (Collection of DeGiorgis and Van Alstyne)

Side chair, ca. 1840. New Lebanon, New York. Fine curly maple. Varnish finish. (Courtesy of David A. Schorsch)

Side chair, ca. 1840. Enfield, Connecticut. A similar pommel to the child's chairs from Enfield, Connecticut. Worn green paint. (The Art Complex of Duxbury)

Side chair, ca. 1840. South Union, Kentucky. Pommel separated from the post by a long neck. Boldly shaped back slats. Typical strong concave taper on the bottom of the posts. Mustard yellow paint. (Mr. and Mrs. Jack Rhodus)

Side chairs, ca. 1840. Enfield, Connecticut. Metal rod used to strengthen the pommel. Tilters on two of the chairs. Exquisite proportions. Strong birdseye and curly maple. Shellac finish. (Private collection. Photograph by Richard D. Meyer)

Armed rocker, ca. 1850. New Lebanon, New York. A fine tall rocker with 5 slats. Side scroll arms. Yellow paint. (Collection of John Keith Russell)

Armed rocker, ca. 1830. Union Village, Ohio. Numerous chairs from Ohio communities were finished with more than one color of paint. Orange and mustard yellow paint. (Mr. and Mrs. Jack Rhodus)

Back of side chair, ca.1820. Repainted late 19th or early 20th century. Worn green, red and yellow paint over original red paint. (Timothy D. Rieman)

Pommel and back slat, ca.1840. South Union, Kentucky. Mustard yellow paint. (Mr. and Mrs. Jack Rhodus)

Tape seat, ca. 1840. Pleasant Hill, Kentucky. Handwoven tape. (Shakertown at Pleasant Hill)

Tape seat, ca.1840. Canterbury, New Hampshire. (Courtesy New York State Museum, Albany, New York)

Tape seat, ca.1840. Pleasant Hill, Kentucky. Handwoven tape. (Shakertown at Pleasant Hill)

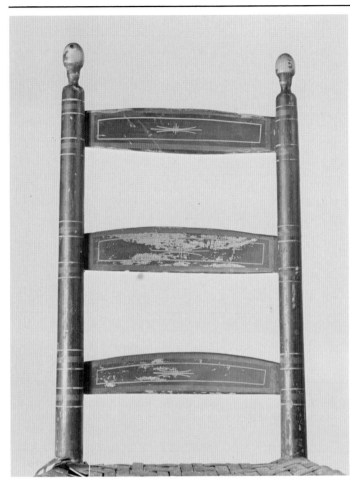

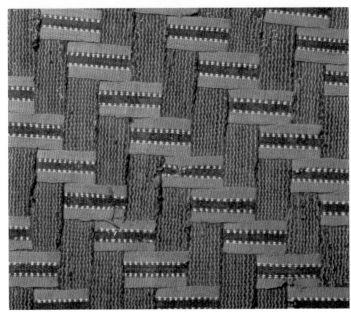

Armed rocker, ca.1840. A bold rocker with unusual rocker blade proportions. Worn gray paint. (Shakertown at Pleasant Hill)

INTRODUCTION

The history and development of the Shaker chair is a statement about the Shakers and their relationship with the world. The United Society of Believers in Christ's Second Appearance is a separatist religious community established in the world, but not of it. Its members have come from the world, bringing materials, skills, and concepts that were changed towards perfection within the community and often returned to the world in the form of improved ideas and products.

While the United Society acknowledged separation from the world, it also depended upon the world for new members and for a market for its products. The slat back chair was abundant during the time of the early and rapid growth of Shaker communities. The form of the slat back chair was refined, produced, and sometimes sold by the Shakers. A hundred years later, this *improved style* became the pattern for a variety of chair companies which sought to imitate the success of the Shaker industry.

Account books and daily records provide evidence that many communities made chairs in the first quarter of the nineteenth century. This production was necessary to meet the needs of the increasing numbers of new residents in the communities. Occasional sales are noted in the account books. Documentation of chair making in written material is limited or non-existent in some communities where chairs are known to have been made, such as Canterbury and Enfield, New Hampshire, North Union, Whitewater and Watervliet, Ohio. In the case of West Union in Indiana, there are account book references to the sale of chairs but known examples are non-existent for this community which closed more than one hundred and fifty years ago. Neither written material nor chairs have been found to document chair making at Hancock, Tyringham,

Shirley, Sodus Bay and Groveland. Since these settlements were close to other communities that produced chairs, there was no necessity to make a product easily obtainable from the neighboring community.

The United Society was structured with each community divided into families of a few to one hundred or more members. These were usually named according to their geographic relationship to the Meeting House. The family living in the area immediately surrounding the Meeting House was called the Church or Center Family. Others were the North, West, South, and East Families. Sometimes the names developed as a result of other factors, such as a distant location (an *outer* family like Upper Canaan) or industry (Mill Family). Each family operated as a separate economic entity. The sale of chairs became a part of this economic structure. As early as 1789, they were being sold, both to other Shaker families and to buyers in the outside world.

From this date to the closing of the chair business in 1942, New Lebanon dominated Shaker chair production, reaching its peak in the last quarter of the nineteenth century when catalogues were widely distributed. At the same time, though, some communities were purchasing furnishings, including chairs, from factories outside the United Society.

From the dual position of being in the world and yet an entity separate from it, the Shaker chair evolved definite design characteristics that related to, but were distinctively different from, those produced by the world's people. The Shaker chair is an outward expression of internal concepts: simplicity, separation from the world, utilitarianism, community, and a dedication to fine craftsmanship. It is a philosophy of life presented in a tangible form; a form that was copied at the end of the nineteenth century, inspired the Danish designers of the 1930s, and is being duplicated by craftspeople across the country today. It is religion applied to America's material culture... the Shaker chair.

THE SHAKER STYLE

Two traditions have dominated the history of chairmaking: that of the joiner working with flat boards held together by the mortise and tenon joint; and that of the turner using the lathe and drill to produce wares often referred to as stick furniture. It is this second tradition that became the foundation for the New England slat back chair and, in turn, the classical Shaker form.

The turner's slat back chair has two front and two back posts connected by parallel stretchers in a box arrangement. Each stretcher connects the legs of the lower section. The seat itself is composed of similar stretchers supporting seating material of rush, tape or list, splint, cane, leather, or cloth. The back of the turner's slat back chair is constructed of one or more slats, usually bent, mortised and fastened into the back posts. Scribe marks on the posts are guides for the

New England slat back chair, ca.1690. (Collections of Greenfield Village and the Henry Ford Museum, Dearborn, Michigan)

New England "Carver" armchair, ca.1650. (Collections of Greenfield Village and the Henry Ford Museum, Dearborn, Michigan)

Highchair. 19th century. Drop scroll arm. (Courtesy of the New Hampshire Historical Society, Concord, New Hampshire)

placement of stretchers and back slats. These are often omitted on machine-produced parts for which jigs provided proper placement.

With few exceptions, the Shaker chair is an adaptation of the New England slat back chair. Many of the design elements of Shaker chairs can be seen in their regional and contemporary counterparts: mushroom-shaped handholds on top of the front posts are refinements of handholds on chairs of the Pilgrim period; the finely shaped, scrolled arms on chairs from Canterbury and Enfield, New Hampshire, are similar to arms appearing on many non-Shaker chairs from New Hampshire, while the Harvard variation is strikingly similar to that attributed to the nearby world communities of Boston and Salem. The influence of the Windsor style is apparent in the revolving chairs, the dining chairs from the New Hampshire communities, and the stretchers of chairs from Alfred.

Although there are a few examples of the work of a clockmaker from before and after he became a Shaker, such information is not available with reference to chairmakers. The changes in a chairmaker's concept of style resulting from his participation in the radically different environment of the Shaker community can not be identified.

The initial domestic needs of the Shakers were met by the new converts who brought their skills, experiences, and household furnishings with them. In 1788, the *Memmo of Movebel Estate of Gideon Turner* includes *1 set carpenters tools and 1 set joiners tools.* The following year, Stephen Slosson, *came to live in this family* (Hancock) *and brought his joiner's tools.* An inventory from 1796 shows that William Parker brought with him a *chair and small chairs,* while the *Personal Effects received of Valentine Rathbone* included *seven chairs.*

As the Shaker communities grew, the importation of styles from the world continued through new members, special needs, or purchases from the world. On January 25, 1821, *Lydia Patridge came here* (Watervliet, New York) *to live.* The *Account of her things that she brought here* included *One Great wheal, one foot wheal, quil wheal and swifts, half a dozen chairs . . .* On June 5, 1857, *Miller went to Schenectady. Got a chair on wheels for Clarissa to move about in.* An account from New Lebanon on March 17, 1825, reports *Nicholas & Garret go in persuit of an easy chair,* and returned three days later from Vermont with one. And listed in the expenses *paid by Martha Pease and Anna in the year 1855* at Enfield, Connecticut, is $12.00 for a *Second hand sofa.*

When the Shakers began producing quantities of chairs at the turn of the nineteenth century, the New England slat back chair had become much simpler than its predecessors. The Shakers simplified the designs even further. Ring turnings are omitted on the back posts, front posts below the seat, and the stretchers. The resulting standardized form consists of back posts devoid of superficial turnings with a well-defined distance between the oval-shaped pommels and the lower section of the posts. Front posts lack embellishment from the seat to the bottom of the posts and do not have turnings to define separate feet.

On armchairs, vase turnings often adorn the front posts between the seat and the arms. The bent back slats generally have a sweeping curve along the top and a straight lower edge. Most rockers are flat and fitted into slots cut into the base of the posts. The style of the arms is a variant of either a flat surface or a shaped drop scroll. This simplification of the turned slat back chair separates the product of the Shaker craftsman from that of his contemporaries. It also offers a uniformity while it permitted diversity between communities.

The highly structured government and communal relationships within the United Society of Believers provided for guidance in the transmission and standardization of design. Records indicate regular trade between individual communities, each often specialized in producing particular items. Hancock purchased chairs from New Lebanon; Enfield, Connecticut, received them from Harvard. A journal from New Lebanon notes that on March 12, 1831, *Daniel Willard and Bennet Bolton start for home* (Shirley) *after dinner with 102 chairs.*

Transfers of leaders and members also contributed to the standardization of design as can be seen in the life of Brother Freegift Wells, whose journal is cited in the following chapter. Brother Freegift lived and worked in Watervliet, New York, from 1803 to 1836 when he moved to Union Village to serve as elder for seven years. Having made chairs in New York, he set up his lathe in Ohio to turn out chairs. He returned to Watervliet and, upon retirement from the eldership, once more engaged in the craft of chairmaking.

Even when the itinerant leader was not a craftsperson, he or she often noted and passed on furniture styles of the communities visited. Such was true of Elder James Prescott of North Union and Elder Henry Blinn from Canterbury who kept daily diaries of their trips.

On some occasions, design information was sought; Elder Benjamin Seth Youngs was building the Center Family dwelling at South Union and wrote to New Lebanon requesting *the form & dimensions of your dining room tables & benches.*

The transmission and standardization of style and the flow of ideas throughout a widespread area were not happenstance. There is evidence that chair design was directed and given approval by the leadership. Presented in this book under the Harvard and Enfield, Connecticut, chapters is a series of letters that discusses the *new fashioned chair . . . which will do for believers to pattern after.* Contained therein are such expressions as *pass upon the . . . improved Pattern, blessed at the fountain head, rocking chair is condemned,* and *the small chair admitted with some modifications.*

For almost a century, the Shaker chair was refined until the chairmakers in the world began to notice and imitate the styles developed by the Believers. The Shakers drew from the world, made improvements, and then gave a finer product back to the world. The evolution of the style of Shaker chairs is the material expression of a faith that called on the Believers to convert the world to a simpler and better way of life.

"The peculiar grace of a Shaker chair is due to the fact that it was made by someone capable of believing that an angel might come and sit on it." (Thomas Menton, introduction to *Religion in Wood* by Edward and Faith Andrews).

January.

1861

Mond 28. Altered the rockers on a small chair for Eliza Ash. Went to the mill & got a cherry plank for posts to a stool chair, also a block for a mallet.

Tues 29. Made a pleating stick out of cherry 4½ feet long for the Tayloresses, & other chours.

Wedn 30. Overhauled my pile of boards & selected stuff for my big chair. Also made a draught of it to work by.

Thur 31. Went to the ciderhouse & brought over some boards to make Eunice's coffin as we do not know how soon she may finish off, being speechless & blind & also deaf as far as we know. I plained out the bottom board & struck a center line upon it & laid it by till it is needed. Made a mallet &c.

February.

Friday 1. Been trying & plaining out stuff for my stool chair &c.

Satur 2. Done up some more plaining & assisted Thomas some in his work.

FREEGIFT WELLS, CHAIRMAKER

The existing journal writings of Freegift Wells have left an extensive and informative record of a Shaker chairmaker. The more than twelve hundred pages relate the daily activities of the author and the Shaker community, including the weather, trips to nearby towns for supplies, eventful Sunday meetings, the raising of build-ings, and many of the mundane daily tasks, such as *cut(ting) up cod-fish for dinner.*

These pages also record the variety of tasks performed by Brother Freegift, the craftsman:

May 13, 1814—...begun a pattern for a trundle-bead...
*August 4, 1814, while visiting New Lebanon—...finished one
    flight of stairs except the hand rail & banisters...*
*November 29, 1814—...finished the pattent treddles and they
    appear to work very well...*
*March 13, 1815—Finished the dippers & the whole number that
    has been made this winter is 540 ...*
December 17, 1819—...finished plaining off 9 nests of boxes...
*January 15, 1820—...turned the pullies for the rolling
    machine...*
August, 1822—...split out 2560 pen handles...
*July 12, 1831—...turned 160 screw for sash casing this fore-
    noon...He turned at the rate of 30 an hour when the lathe
    was in operation*
October 3, 1831—... rivoted the chairs springs together ...
October 8, 1831—... finished Samuels coffin ...
June 6, 1861—...strung 100 broom handles...
February 10, 1866—Mended a great chair which I broke.

It is as though Brother Freegift always remembered the admonition which he recorded on a *very pleasant* Thanksgiving day in 1819: *Samuel administered a gift to the family from Mother which is for us to wake up & be sharp & zealous in hand labour.*

Freegift Wells was born in Southold, Suffolk, New York, on May 20, 1785. In *A Concise Essay* written by him on August 11, 1865, he offered a brief insight into his home and referred to his coming to the Shakers.

As I was my parents youngest child, I remained with them nearly a year after all the rest of their children (nine in number) had left them, and found homes by themselves, which, I had no doubt yielded them more satisfactory enjoyment than they could possibly have realized if they had remained with their Parents. . . . Having made all necessary arrangements, I started for the Land of promise, May 6th 1803, and arrived (I think) on the 17th . . .

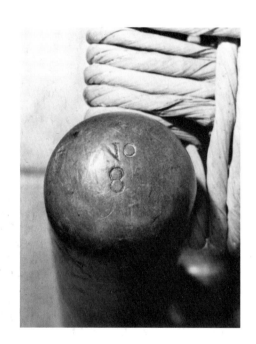

Brother Freegift spent the remaining 67 years of his life as a Shaker, many of those years as a craftsman and elder, and died in Watervliet, New York, on April 15, 1871.

The activities of Brother Freegift as a chairmaker are well documented from 1814 to 1830 and, again, from 1857 to 1864. One of the earliest chairmaking entries was on March 31, 1814 when he *bent the backs for 2 waggon chair,* while *Nathan Slosson has been making a spring for the chairs.* On September 27, 1819, he *began to trim off & ball the chairs.* The next month, on the 19th, he *finished off balling the new chairs.* These are the earliest known references to what are today called *tilters.*

A notation that appears in his journals and contributes significantly to an understanding of Shaker chairs was recorded on Saturday, November 27, 1819. Brother Freegift *has been sorting over & marking chairs. The chairs in the Deacons room are marked 1, the Deaconeses room 2, the Brethern's meeting room 3, the Sisters meeting room 4, the Bretherns front chamber 5, the Sisters front chamber 6, the Brethrens north chamber 7, the Sisters north chamber 8, etc.* This reference indicates the use of a numbering system for the assigning and placement of chairs to specific rooms.

Brother Freegift worked on sizable numbers of chairs from 1818 to 1820, 1824 to 1825, and in the early 1830s before moving to Union Village. Having served as an elder of the Church Family at Watervliet, he left for the Ohio community with Brother Rufus Bishop reading a farewell address *to the young at Watervliet* on May 8, 1836.

The journals covering the years of his leadership in Ohio record his chairmaking there. Additionally, the journal of Elder James S. Prescott of North Union, visiting Union Village on October 1, 1842, noted: *This morning Elder Freegift came over after us to go over to his shop & make a visit. Elder Br. and I went over & staid an hour or two . . . Elder Freegift showed us his Turning Lathe, Shop & work Bench that he made himself and the like . . .*

After leaving his position of leadership in Ohio, Brother Freegift returned to Watervliet, New York. He went to Albany on July 22, 1857, *to get a clock repaired, and to get him some joiner tools.* On May 6, 1858, D.A. Buckingham recorded in his journal that *Br. Freegift is to work fixing up a turning Lathe at the mill.* On May 2, 1859, Brother Freegift made the following notation in his journal:

In commemoration of the 2nd anniversary of my releasement from the office of Elder Brother of this family, I have started my new buz saw in my lathe room & it bids fair to do a tolerable good business when we get the belts softened up so that they will not slip on the pullys. Then, on January 30, 1861, at the age of seventy-five, Brother Freegift began devoting much of his time to his craft as chairmaker: *. . . over hauled my pile of boards & selected stuff for my big chair. Also made a daught of it to work by.*

The preparation and production of chairs during the last decade of Brother Freegift's life work are well delineated in his journals and explicitly depict the chairmaking process.

February.

1861.

Mon 4. Plained out my chair posts & did some other plaining.

Tues 5. Plained some & turned some, & afternoon cut up near 30 fish ready ~~fry~~ for frying and boiling.

Wedn 6. Helped to get the morticing machine from the mill to the shop, took it to piece, & cleaned it all up, & did up some morticing &c.

Thur 7. Worked some at my chair this forenoon, Afternoon began to make a coffin for Eunice.

Friday 8. Worked all day at the coffin.

Satur 9. Finished the coffin about 10 Oclock and put the corpse into it.

Mon 11. , finished mortising my chair posts this forenoon. Afternoon went to the mill & helped Elder Daniel buz out partitions for seed boxes.

Tues'd 12. Went to the mill again & finished sawing Elder Daniels box partitions.

Wedn 13. Went to the mill again & turned out my chair post, & some other chair Chancey returned home, having been gone 6 weeks

In the material that follows, the left-hand italicized column contains excerpts from the 1861-1863 journals of Brother Freegift. The right-hand column is a combination of excerpts from his other journals and explanatory comments by the authors of this book.

November 1861

Friday 29   Cut up chair-rounds to the right length for turning . . .

April 28, 1830—*Elder Br. & Freegift have been buzzing up lumber for chair rounds.*

December 1861

Tues 3   Finished cutting up chair-rounds and had enough for 96 chairs.

Thurs 5   Went to the Mill and tried out chair rounds, so as to square them with the buz saw.

Satur 7   Been buzing chair-round stuff all day, slitting up, and taking them to a size ready for the lathe, but have considerable more to do yet in the same line.

The process of making chair parts began with planks that had been cut from timber or logs with the buzz saw. These boards were then cut or split, perhaps riven, along the grain so the grain in the rounds (rungs or stretchers) would follow the length of the rounds. These pieces were shaped by use of the buzz saw and/or planes to square the pieces of wood suitable for turning. This stock was then cut, again on the buzz saw, to the appropriate length for the rounds.

Wedne 18   Went to the Mill and contrived some about turning chair-rounds.

Friday 20   Went to Albany with Jesse . . . Bought me a couple of chair bits.

Tuesd 31   Went to the Mill and sorted over and counted all my chair rounds which was buzed out and found that there lacked 9 long rounds and 25 short ones

to complete the com-
pliment for a 100 chairs.

January 1862

Friday 10   *Went to the Mill and hunted*
up some more stuff and
sawed to the length a full
compliment for the rounds
for 100 chairs. Afternoon
repaired a two story foot
bench for Samantha.

Tuesd 14   *Worked some at a frame*
and jaws for turning chair-
rounds.

Most chairmaking processes were ideally suited for mass production. Making a jig or setting up a lathe like the one Brother Freegift used took considerably longer than the actual making of the part itself. Once the preparation had been completed, the production went quickly.

March 4, 1830—*F has been turning chair rounds. turned 50 in 32 minutes.*

January 20, 1824—*rough turned 100 chair round in 55 minutes.*

January 21, 1824—*F continued to turn chair rounds. turned 100 in 36½ minutes.*

April 23, 1819— *We finished turning chair posts with the machine having turned enough for 102 chairs in two days. We turned 15 long posts in 14 minutes . . .*

February 1862

Mond 3   *Made a machine for*
centering chair-rounds and
centered 100 with it.

Tuesd 4   *Centered 300 more today.*
The labor of plaining the
ends of those which are
rather too large to bring
them to the right size, is
more than the centering.

The wood used for the chair rounds had to be accurately centered in the lathe for proper turning. Brother Freegift built a jig or machine to quickly find the center-point on the ends of the chair rounds and then mark that point in preparation for chucking in the lathe. With the help of this mechanism, the centering was quickly and easily performed.

Thur 20   *Went to the Mill and did*
something at fitting my
chair round frame on the
lathe bench . . . also
ground up all my largest
lathe tools.

March 1862

Mon 3   *Thomas cleaned up all the*
boxes and gudgeons in
the lathe room which was
a real job.

Thomas was Brother Freegift's helper in the shop and often performed the less skilled tasks. The term "gudgeons" was used by Brother Freegift in two contexts.

In this instance, it is probably in reference to the bearings for the line shaft system which drove the lathe. A second useage of the term appears in the March 24, 1862, notation referring to turning down the ends of the chair rounds to form tenons.

Mond 10   *Went to Albany and bought a small chain for the chair-round lathe and some other things.*

Wedn 12   *Went to the Mill fitted the chain instead of a cord and turned 75 rounds before noon and 200 afternoon, it works well.*

Thur 13   *Turned rounds again today, I believe about 400*

February 5, 1819—*F turned 250 chair rounds.*

Friday 14   *Turned again this forenoon, and 100 after dinner. Then buzed some for Br. Austin and George, Also turned rounds for George. We found we could turn 100 chair-rounds in less than an hour.*

February 27, 1819—*F. Finished turning chair rounds.*

Satur 15   *Today we finished turning our chair rounds about 1000, nearly finished before noon. A short time before we finished the machine working very complete, we counted out 25 sticks and turned them very complete in 7 minutes, which was four over three per minute.*

Tuesd 18   *Forenoon worked at broom handles. Afternoon worked at altering my chair round frame and boxes, for the purpose of turning some tapering rounds for backs to a couple long chairs, one in the meeting room, and one in the Physicians shop.*

Numerous journal references in 1862 suggest that a duplicating lathe was used by Brother Freegift which could make simple turnings, such as a chair round, in less than twenty seconds and a chair post in less than one minute. This lathe, like many of the "improved" lathes patented and produced by non-Shaker manufacturers of the period, had the cutters held by a part of the machine rather than by the turner. Called the "box" (August 9 and 21), this part could hold several cutters and was moved along the runway (August 19) from the tailstock towards the headstock.

The movement was governed manually, by means of a screw feed, or with weights using cord or chain (March 10, 12). One cutter was probably fixed and cut the square or octagon-shaped wood stock to a round dowel shape. A second cutter, probably moveable, cut the basic form such as the convex taper on chair rounds, the long taper on the top half of the rear posts, or the taper on the bottom of the front posts.

Wedn 19 *Been at work at the mill grinding and leveling off the bottoms of the lathe rests so that they will set level on the bench which hitherto had not been effected.*

Satur 22 *Went to the mill this forenoon and fixed up for turning gudgeons on chair-rounds.*

Mond 24 *Made a beginning to gudgeon chair rounds and finished off 80.*

Here Brother Freegift turned the grudgeons or tenons on each end of the chair rungs.

Mon 31 *Turned 150 chair rounds.*

April 1862

Thur' 3 *Turned 33 chair rounds which finished the 1000 which I had on hand.*

February 12, 1819—*F. finished turning chair rounds the first time over.* A week later, he *turned the tenons of 150 chair rounds, a good days work.* The chair rounds were first turned on the lathe from the wood stock. They were later re-chucked and the gudgeons or tenons cut at the ends of the rounds so as to fit into the bored holes.

Friday 4 *Worked at altering my frame for turning tapering rounds for the back of a long chair at the head of the meeting in our meeting room. And also for a sort of settee for Jannet at the Physician's shop.*

Mon 7 *Went into the east woods and hunted up a maple tree for chair backs. Thomas cut it down and we trimed it out and sawed up the logs and got home to dinner.*

Maple was the wood most consistently used for making chairs. On April 7, 1819, Brother Freegift recorded: *Elder Br. & F. went & cut maple log on Shellys land for chair posts and got it to the mill.* As noted in a January 6, 1825, reference, they often had to travel some distance to obtain proper materials: *Nathan Spier & William (Bates) have been after lumber for chair posts over the Mohawk (River).*

Friday 11 *Worked again at repairing the old buz saw frame and setting up the cross cut for sawing the backs and posts to length.*

Satur 12	Sawed up our plank for chair backs into their lengths in the forenoon.	February 12, 1825—*William B has been sawing out plank for chair posts.*
Mond 14	Worked at the mill sawing and buzzing out slats for chair backs.	
Wedn' 16	Buzed up a quantity of maple plank into strips for chair posts.	The sawn material was stacked in an attic space for drying.
Friday 18	Stuck up my chair post stuff in the lumber room in the lower loft.	
Satur' 19	Stuck up my chair back stuff in the north garret of the dwelling house under the tin roof.	
Thur' 24	Worked the most of the day at my frame for turning chair posts.	

May 1862

Thur' 8	Brought my old frame for boreing chairs on from the ciderhouse garret, Found it all shackling and entirely unfit for use. Been repairing it, and trying to fit a brace and bit to conform to it.	March 17, 1819—*F. finished the machine for boreing chair posts.* The frame held a brace and bit at the proper angles to drill the chair posts for receiving the rounds.
Satur' 10	Been hunting up some old racks for bending chair backs.	The back slats were steamed (July 25, 1862) to permit the wood to be bent. They were then placed in a rack or frame which would hold the slats while drying in their bent form (November 5, 1862).
Mond 12	Went to Albany with Jesse bought a plank for a seat in the Meeting room.	
Wednes 21	Worked at my bit and brace, and Thomas at racks for bending chair backs.	
Friday 23	Finished my frame and bit for boreing chair posts.	
Friday 30	Worked at my plank chair again and nearly finished	

*the seat part, but have
the back and legs to make
yet.*

June 1862

Thurs 5   *. . . Went to the Mill and
turned the 4 legs for the
Meeting R bench also
turned the ends of 30 back
rounds.*

Friday 13   *Plained out, bored and
finished off the long back
or top pieces to the
Ministry and Elders chair
in the Meeting room.*

Satur' 14   *. . . finished off the long
chair . . .*

Wed 25   *Sawed out some stuff for a
box for the mortising
chair posts.*

This box was probably a jig for holding the chair posts at the proper angle as they were mortised to receive the back slats.

Friday 27   *Went to Albany with Jesse
and made a contract for
plaining my chair backs
to a thickness.*

December 21, 1818—*F. split 185 chair backs.*

Mon 30   *Finished smoothing out
chair backs and packed
them up in boxes to take
to Albany for running
thru' the plaining machine
to bring them to thickness.*

Brother Freegift attempted to get the back slats planed to the proper thickness in nearby Albany. The machines mentioned in his journals consisted of a buzz saw, several lathes . . . one for metal . . . and a mortising machine, but no planers. These machines were, at various times, driven by water, wind and, possibly, steam.

July 1862

Satur' 5   *Went to the mill and carried
off all the short wood and
turning chips from our
lathe and buz saw, and
Thomas turned two stools
and their legs, for milking
stools this forenoon;*

Satur 12   *Went to Albany with
Channey to get my chair
backs plained, but the
man's machine could not
do the work, and we took
them to Velie's Bedstead
factory and left them to
await Viely's decision who
was not there.*

Thur 17	*Towards night we prepared for plaining our chair backs to a thickness, having failed to get them done in Albany.*
Friday 18	*Worked nearly all day at plaining chair backs and it proves to be quite hard work for the old man's hand and arm.*
Satu' 19	*Yesterday and today we have planed 200 chair backs.*
Friday 25	*Worked at broom handles till about 10 o'clock . . . then took our chair-back stuff over to the wash house and made preparations for bending after dinner. Then afternoon we steamed and bent about 300 chair backs and got done before supper.*
Mon' 28	*Went to the Mill and moved all our chair post timber from the celler to our buz-room loft, sorted it over and took a large portion of them to their length.*
Tuesd' 29	*Finished taking our chair posts to a length till our stuff failed and to make up a compliament of each sort, I went into the woods and Thomas fell a small tree but it proved to poor to answer our purpose.*
Wedn' 30	*Went into the woods and found a small tree which had been struck by lightening and broken down, the stuff was handsome and we got it home and cut it to the lengths we wanted, split it out and had a plenty to make our present compliment.*
Thur' 31	*Buzed out the stuff we got yesterday into lengths for*

Not being able to have the chair back slats properly planed in Albany, Brother Freegift undertook to perform the task with hand tools.

December 26, 1818—*F. shaved out 100 chair backs.*

April 12, 1819—*Eld br. N & F. went to buzzing up chair posts.*

chair posts so that we now have a full compliment of stuff to make 86 chairs, and backs and rounds enough to make a 100 at this time, but leave the 14 for another job.

August 1862

Friday 1 *Yesterday and today we have buzed over all our posts and brought them to the exact size we want them for turning.*

Mon' 4 *Forenoon worked in the shop at a chuck and fixture for cornering chair posts, afternoon cornered 344 with (the buzz saw).*

April 13, 1819—. . . *we have been buzzing & cornering chair posts.*

"Cornering" was the process of cutting off the corners of the square wood stock to make the pieces octagon shaped, or more nearly round. In this way, less wood needed to be removed in the turning process and that operation becomes more smoothly and quickly performed.

Wedn' 6 *Spent nearly all day in trying to turn chair posts, but could not make good work of it till later in the afternoon when we turned 12 or 14 so they would answer.*

Thur' 7 *Trying to turn again, posts so seasoned makes a hard case of it, turned a few, and concluded we must saw them tapering which work we commence.*

Wood turning is easier if the wood retains some of its "growth" moisture. The seasoned wood was very hard and difficult to cut on the lathe. Therefore, excess wood was sawn from the stock so that a lesser amount would have to be removed on the lathe as the posts were tapered from the seat up.

Satur' 9 *Finished tapering and began to turn again and found we could turn much better, but our boxes which were of wood wore out and we had to line them with brass. This was quite a hinderance and we were not able to rough turn all our posts.*

Mon' 11 *Got all our chair posts thro' the lathe the first time over*

April 22, 1819—*El Br and F. Began to turn chair posts again & this afternoon turned one hundred . . .*

Friday 15 *Not much done by me today,*

however I went to the Mill and buzed out some stuff to make a new box for turning chair posts, for we have got to turn them all over again.

Mond 18   *Began to make my new tool for turning chair posts.*

Tuesday 19   *Worked all day at repairing the runway of my lathe for turning chair posts.*

Wedn' 20   *Worked all day at my new box and runway*

Thur 21   *Worked all day at my boxes, fitting the places for the cutters, etc.*

Friday 22   *Nearly finished my tool for turning chair posts.*

Satur' 23   *Have nearly finished my boxes and cast 3 weights to attach to them etc.*

Mon' 25   *Worked at my follower and lead weights the chief part of the day.*

Wedn' 27   *Finished my lathe works this forenoon, except grinding up the new irons. Afternoon to my frame to the mill, fixed it on the lathe bench; ground the irons etc.*

Thurs' 28   *Made some beginning to turn chair posts over the second time, but had poor luck, and found we must fix some more.*

Friday 29   *Tried again and made out better till every point of our chuck broke which cost near a half days work to repair.*

Satur' 30   *Began again this morning and had good luck, and finished turning all our short posts, and they are well done.*

September 1862

Mond' 1   *Began to turn long posts this morning and turned perhaps two thirds of them*

Tues' 2   *Finished turning our long posts this forenoon, After- noon cleaned out our lathe and buz room, barrelled up shavings and edgings, and did a little buzing, etc.*

Wedn' 3   *Worked mostly in the shop fixing matters preparitory to turning pummels.*

Just as the chair rounds had to be centered into the lathe a second time for the turning of the tenons, the rear posts had to be re-centered for the turning of the pommels at a later time. This process was probably performed by hand on a standard lathe.

Friday 5   *. . . turned 30 pommels to the long chair posts.*

April 24, 1819—*F. began to turn the ends of the long chair posts & turned 68 . . .*

Mon' 8   *Afternoon worked some in the shop, and turned 12 great chair pommels*

Thur' 11   *Finished turning pommels, being in all about 170.*

Friday 12   *Turned about one half of the front posts.*

Satur' 13   *Turned about 40 short posts this forenoon, and this makes a finish of turning chair posts.*

Mon 15   *Went to the mill and buzed off the lower ends of all the chair posts.*

Tuesd' 30   *Made a sort of box for gaging and mortising chair posts in.*

"Gaging" may have been the mea- suring, laying out, and marking with a scribe line the locations on the posts where the holes for stretchers and back slats were to be located.

Wed' 1   *Worked at my augur, and boreing machine for boreing chair posts, etc.*

Wedne' 8   *Dressed off chair backs and smothed a few posts and undertook to mortice them but had bad luck, and had to repair the machinery before I could succeed.*

Thur 9   *Dressed out some chair backs and smoothed off some chair posts.*

Satur' 11   *Worked again in my chair business bored one ready for driving together.*

Mon' 13   *Got my first chair together today, and finished it off.*

Thur' 30   *Went to Albany and bought a number of small articles that I wanted. Among the rest I got six pence worth of terredecene to use as an experiment for staining chairs.*

November 1862

Satur' 1   *Worked at chairs again today, and got one together.*

March 30, 1819—*F finished boring posts for 20 chairs & put one together . . .*

Wedn' 5   *. . . took the chair backs out of the racks and piled them away in a box.*

Satur' 8   *Worked at chair backs today, but my right arm paines me so that I can hardly work, or write with it.*

Mon' 10   *Worked what I was able at chairs again, finishing off backs, sand papering posts etc.*

Tues 11   *Morticed 10 chair posts in the machine and had some trouble with my chisel, had to have it hardened over etc.*

Wednes' 12   *Cleaned out my mortices and made some beginning to bore.*

Satur 15   *Drive 5 chairs together and they are finished except levelling the bottoms.*

April 6, 1819—*F finished off 5 more chairs.*

Mon 17   *Trimmed 5 chairs which was put together saturday, and worked some at backs.*

Thur' 20   *Buzed 60 chair backs, took them to an exact length and rounded the upper side, etc.*

Friday 28   *Finished off backs enough for 20 chairs except sand papering.*

December 1862

Mon 1   *Sand papered chair backs and filed and sandpapered chair posts.*

Mond' 8   *Morticed chair posts this forenoon.*

Wed. 10   *Bored and drive 16 chair fronts together.*

Thur 11   *. . . bored and drove together 6 chair fronts.*

Tuesd 16   *Put chair backs together.*

Slat back chairs were assembled in two separate units, front and back, with the side stretchers then joining these to form the chair. On this Thursday, Brother Freegift completed the front units which consisted of two front posts and three stretchers. The following Tuesday, he began to put together the back sections which consisted of the two rear posts, two stretchers, and several back slats (February 20, 1863). Stretchers then joined the front and back sections to form the chair frame (February 27, 1863).

Thur' 18   *Pinned off chair backs and trimmed them.*

The mortise and tenon joints of the back slats with the rear posts were usually fastened with wood pins inserted through the posts and the ends of the slats. The extra length of the pins protruding on the back side of the posts was trimmed even with the posts. Today, the shrinkage that has occurred over the years across the grain of the posts usually leaves these pins protruding again. On the chairs of Brother Freegift, as is true of most Shaker chairs, only the top slats are pinned. This keeps the posts from pulling apart at the top.

Satur 20   Been at work at a bench for putting chairs together on, having had nothing heavy enough.

Tues 23   Been centering and beginning the holes in near 20 chairs.

Wedn' 24   Bored and drove together 20 chairs, which together with the 10 already finished makes 30 ready for staining except leveling the bottoms of the posts.

Mond' 29   Did a little about fixing some stain for chairs.

January 1863

Friday 2   Sorted over the chair backs and picked out a lot for 29 chairs and began to work at them

Satur' 3   Scraped over all my lot of chair backs and marked off about a quarter of them with the pattern on both sides.

Mond 5   Marked our chair backs this forenoon, afternoon went to the Mill, filed the small buz saw and tenoned about half the backs and rounded about a quarter of them.

The ends of the slats were tenoned or reduced in thickness or width in order to fit tightly into the mortises of the rear posts.

Tuesd 6   Marked off chair backs again. Afternoon went to the Mill and tenoned them and rounded the top edge of them all.

Wedn' 7   Worked at dressing the top

*edge of the backs and cut
up cod-fish for dinner.*

Wedn' 14   *Worked at long posts today,
fileing those that needed
it and began to mortice.*

Thur 15   *Morticed 10 posts . . .*

Tues 20   *Today finished morticing
my batch of posts 56 in
number.*

Thur' 22   *Been putting chair backs
together, got the eleven
short backs for the Office
together.*

Friday 23   *Put 15 chair backs together
and had good luck.*

Monday 26   *Went to albany with Jesse
and got some paints for
staining chairs.*

Thurs 29   *Set out my front and part
of my back posts and
began the holes and made
ready for the machine.*

Saturday 31   *Finished boreing my posts
and drove them all together.
I have now 28 chairs of
the last batch, which
added to the 30 before
finished makes 58*

February 1863

Wedn 4   *Having finished off the 58
chairs we took them all to
the dye-house chamber
where the sisters are to
stain them.*

In the journal writings of 1819, Brother Freegift described the finishing processes of those early years.

October 15—*F & two sisters stained 35 chairs with aquefortes . . .*

October 16—*Eld Br. & F. & Ward built an oven for heating chairs.*

October 17—*Eld Br. & F. heat 33 chairs in our new oven & give them a handsome color.*

November 18—*F & 3 sisters have rub'd & oil'd 34 chairs.*

November 26—*F & the sisters rub'd over the chairs & now they are all ready for bottoming.*

Thur' 5 I have taken another batch of posts 38 in number, being all of the middle kind and have straitened, and filed the rough places, so that they are now ready for Thomas to sandpaper etc.

Fri 6 Worked at chair posts and chair backs. the Sisters have stained the 58 chairs we carried over to the dye house Wednesday.

Mon 9 Been to the Mill and sawed my backs to length, tenoned them and ground the upper edge.

Friday 20 I have been putting the back sides of the chairs together - posts, back slats, and rounds.

Fri 27 Boreing chair posts sides ready for driving in the last rounds, and finishing the chair.

March 1863

Tues 3 Leveled off the bottoms of my chairs, so that they are now finished, making in all that are now finished 76 in number, being all of the small chairs that I have posts for.

September 27, 1819—F. began to trim off & ball the chairs.

Monday 16 Sorted over and worked some at my great chair backs.

Tues' 17 Made 3 back patterns and marked off all my backs, about 3 oclock went to the mill and buzed them into shape.

Having completed 76 *small chairs*, Freegift began work on *great chairs* which are armed chairs, usually armed rockers. These chairs probably had graduated back slats and required a separate pattern for each of the three slats.

Friday 27 Drove the rest of my great chairs together, being 6 in all, and they only lack arms, and rockers to make a complete finish.

Mon' 30   Began to repair Archibald's
             great chair, put up a mess
             of haddock for dinner
             fixed a time piece.

April 1863

Thur' 2   Went to the mill to hunt
             up stuff. Afternoon got
             out stuff for rockers, and
             Thomas tried them out,
             12 in number.

Friday 3   Went to the mill and jointed
             my rockers and took them
             to a thickness with the
             buz.

Friday 24 Layed out and cut the rabits
             on the bottons of the
             posts of the four other
             great chairs which are
             now ready for receiving
             the rockers.

Wedn' 29   Worked at sawing out arms
             and the like . . .

May 1863

Tues' 12   Put on two or three pairs of
             arms to my great
             chairs.

Wedn' 13   Finished arming the great
             chairs except pinning them
             to the back posts.

Friday 22 Finished off my great
             chairs and carried them to
             the red wood house. Then
             made a beginning to work
             at Jennets Settee.

After more than one and a half years, Brother Freegift and Thomas have completed the task of making chair frames. While there are no journal entries in the 1860s to the seating of chairs, earlier recordings acknowledge Freegift's familiarity with the process.

Jan. 31, 1820—*Abijah, F & Timothy went over beyond Truaxes after stuff for chair bottoms.*

March 15, 1820—*Eld. Br & F have saw'd out & buzzed up another ash log for chair bottoms.*

Dec. 23, 1819—*Eld Br has been pounding out chair bottom stuff.*

Mar 24, 1820—*F. Finished bottoming the last of the chairs for the new house except for the back garret, having bottomed 56 and David 24 which makes 80 in number.*

Satur' 23 Turned 23 pins for Jennets
settee and glued and
pinned the front piece.

Tuesd 26 Fixed for turning and turned
29 rounds for the Settee
and a part of the legs.

Thur' 28 Worked at Settee, bored the
seat and glued in the legs.

Friday 29 Fitted in all the rounds,
plained out and bore the
top piece.

Satur' 30 Glued in my rounds, finished
off the top piece and put
it on the rounds in its
place but did not have
time to glue it on.

Tuesd 2 Finished off Jenetts Settee
so that job is now
through with much to my
releasement.

Brother Freegift started to make two *long chairs* in March 1862. One for the meeting room was finished in three months. The second, for Sister Jenett in the Physicians Shop, did not get completed for almost another year. On another occasion, June 6, 1861, Brother Freegift had also performed some work involving Sister Jenett: *Made a 4 light sash for the 2nd house, not to say for Jenett as I have not the honor of making anything for her . . .*

WATERVLIET, NEW YORK

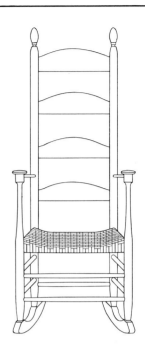

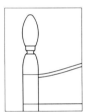
The proximity of Watervliet to New Lebanon suggests a ready flow of persons and products between these two communities. In relation to chairs, this can be noted in two references to Ezra Bishop of New Lebanon. A Watervliet journal records that on August 10, 1814, he *comes and fetches 18 chares.* On a later visit, March 29, 1815, *Ezra Bishop comes from Lebanon, and brings a great chair for John Spier and a number of small ones from the Second family* . . . It is, therefore, easy to understand that there are similarities between the early chairs of New Lebanon and Watervliet, and to appreciate the difficulty in designating a specific community of origin.

Extensive journal records of Watervliet are in the hand of Elder Freegift Wells, the primary chairmaker of that community. Excerpts from those journals describe the manufacture of chairs and are contained in the previous chapter on *Freegift Wells, Chairmaker.* A reading of that material offers an account of chairmaking at Watervliet.

The chairs from this New York community possess pommels that are elliptical in shape with slightly rounded tops. At the lower ends, collars gradually reduce the diameter and descend to narrow necks. Though the shoulders are well-defined, there is a gradual increase in diameter of the posts until reaching the scribe marks for the top slats.

The straight rear posts often terminate in ¾-sphere ball tilters. The bottom of the front posts have a convex taper. The slats on Watervliet chairs are usually chamfered on the front of the top edges.

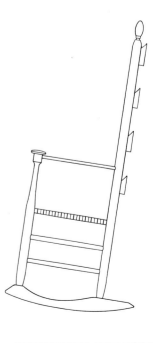

The tops of the rear posts on some dining chairs terminate in minute dome-shaped central turnings located atop sharply formed shoulders with scribe lines immediately below. The classical elliptical pommels are absent on these chairs. The posts gently taper from the shoulder to the bottom of the single wide slat. The high contour of the slat has a distinct chamfer on the top edge. The bottoms of the posts have convex tapers.

Stereo view card, ca. 1880. Clark Photographer. Sisters seated in side chairs. This pommel style is characteristic of Watervliet. (Courtesy of Hancock Shaker Village Inc., Pittsfield, Massachusetts)

While splint is often found as the seating material on Watervliet chairs, tape was also used. A journal reference for April 18, 1814, notes that *the Elders moved the tape loom into the north shop. The Record and Journal of the Sisters written in the First Order at Watervliet* records 1,095 yards of tape woven by the sisters in 1835, 3,166 yards woven in 1836, 855 yards woven in 1837, 1,270 yards woven in 1838, and 733 yards woven in 1839.

Two late references in *Records of the Church at Watervliet, N.Y.* indicate the continual willingness to bring in chairs from outside the Watervliet community. The first is recorded on June 4, 1857, when *Miller went to Schenectady. Got a chair with wheels for Clarissa to move about in.* The second notes that Brother Robert Wagan of the South Family in New Lebanon arrived in February of 1866 *with some chairs for the office here and some for our Sec. Order.*

CLARK, Photographer,

" . . . The Elders rooms were supplied with new chairs today, 5 in each room."

December 7, 1819
Records of the Church at Watervliet, N.Y.

Side chair, ca. 1830. A stocky early side chair. The characteristic Watervliet pommel and beveled back slat was not developed in this early chair. Old splint seat. Red paint. (Courtesy of the New York State Museum, Albany, New York)

Side chair, ca.1840. Characteristic Watervliet pommel and strongly beveled graduated back slats. Rear post notably rounded from top slat to shoulder. Old splint seat. Chrome yellow paint. Similar chair style to those in the Clark stereo view card. (Private Collection)

Side chair, ca. 1840. Date and *sick* marked on front posts. *Sick* probably designates use to the infirmary. Tilters. Old splint seat. (The Sherman Collection)

These chairs with virtually identical pommels and back slats can be attributed to the same unknown maker.

Side chair, ca.1850. Finely detailed side chair. Sister Anna Case gave this chair to Dr. William Olin Stillman who tended to the Shakers in their later years at Watervliet. (Mr. and Mrs. Richard Hehir)

Armed Rocker, ca.1850. Crisply shaped slender arms beveled on both the inside and outside edges. Unusual turning on front post. Mixed woods, maple and probably walnut. (Courtesy of Richard and Betty Ann Rasso)

Side chair, ca.1840. Marked FW on the front post. Probably made by Freegift Wells. Short pommel. Square top edge on minimally graduated backslats. (Douglas and Cornelia Hamel)

Armed rocker, ca.1830. Probably by Free-gift Wells. Old paint. Note the similarity to the rocker style on the previous page. (Courtesy of Hancock Shaker Village Inc., Pittsfield, Massachusetts)

Group of Shakers, ca.1870. Irving photographer, Troy, New York. The photograph helps to verify attributions of Watervliet chairs. Note the unusual lowback chair with pommels at the far left. (Courtesy of the New York State Museum, Albany, New York)

Low back chair, ca.1850. Traditionally used as a dining chair. One journal account refers to a low back chair made for the office. It is rare to find a low back chair with a full pommel. (Courtesy of Hancock Shaker Village Inc. Pittsfield, Massachusetts)

Low back chair, ca.1860-80. Dining chair. The late date of manufacture is noted because of the unusual Victorian period turnings on the front stretcher. Rear posts notably tapered above the strongly beveled back slat. Old splint seat. This style of low back post made without a pommel was made in Watervliet and New Lebanon, New York. (Courtesy of The Shaker Museum, Old Chatham, New York)

ENFIELD, NEW HAMPSHIRE

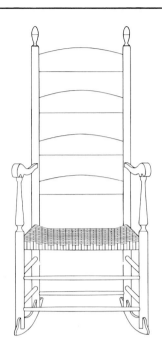

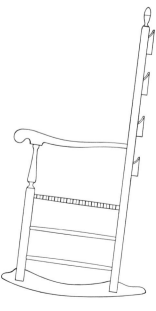

The symmetrical pommel turnings, slender posts, and backward cant make the Enfield chair the most delicate and beautiful of Shaker seating furniture. It is the ultimate expression of the conservation of materials to create a functional form.

Since the location of most of the journals and account books is unknown, the manuscript material provides little information on chairmaking at Enfield. The journal of Elder Henry Blinn, Volume II, lists *James Johnson* as *a good wood workman. . . skilful. . . at the turning lathe.* Ruben Dickey, James Jewett, Jr., and Harvey K. Annis are also mentioned as workmen in wood. But references to the making of chairs are lacking. The unknown author of the 1858 journal said: *Our only resource seem to be, to get what we can from some few old records, which have been kept, and the rest we must gather from those of the aged, who are still left with us.* In the case of chairs, the existing chairs themselves have become the primary source for study.

One occasion which warranted the production of a large number of chairs was the construction of the great stone dwelling. On May 5, 1841, a letter addressed to the *Dearly beloved & much esteemed ministry* contained the following paragraph:

> *We expect the new Stone house, will be so far finished, that it may be wholly occupied in the course of next month, except the kitchen which probably will require more time, to put in the sinks and getting in the water. It is wholly painted, and the pins & knobbs are all put in. The tables are made. The chairs will soon be finished. The stair carpets will soon be put down and lamps hung in the meeting room. So that we have little doubt if our good Friends should visit us this season they will see it nearly completed.*

Hervey Elkins in *Fifteen Years in the Senior Order of Shakers* describes Enfield as having *plain chairs, bottomed with ratten or*

rush, and light so as to be easily portable. . . The post diameters measure a light 1⅛ inches and are made even more slender by a taper extending from the seat. The bottom of the posts possess a taper as they meet the floor. The cane or rattan found on most chairs today contributes to the lightness referred to by Elkins.

The pommels are elongated ellipses with medial scribe marks indicating the thickest diameter of the turning. From this point, the diameter uniformly decreases until terminating in a sharp point at the top and beginning the transition to the neck at the bottom. The neck continues in a smooth and graceful curve to a small ridge that leads to the finely rounded shoulders.

The back slats on Enfield chairs show noticeable width and possess a strong and consistent arch. They are strongly graduated with the widest slat being on the top. This graduation is seen at the point where the slats enter the posts as well as in the center height. The top front edge of the slats are nicely rounded. Only the top slat is secured into the posts with wooden pins from the back.

On rocking chairs, the front posts are very slender and have a vase turning between the seat and the arms. This turning is created by the breaking of the curve of the support with an inward turning rather than being smoothly shaped such as the vase turnings on Canterbury chairs. The posts have a swell turning or collar before being mortised into a blocked section of the arms immediately behind the drop-scrolled handholds.

The arms extend from their mortise at the back posts and flow gracefully downward and then upward over the front posts where the handholds are formed. The underside of the handhold circle and terminate at the block supports. Between the posts, the curve underneath the arms nearly duplicates that on the top. The arms narrow as they extend from the front to the back.

The rockers on Enfield chairs have a sweeping curve across the top between the posts and a concave/convex front edge. The extension of the rockers behind the back posts also have the concave/convex shape but twice the length.

Most of the armless chairs from Enfield have had their back posts drilled for tilters. Even the rocking chairs have hollowed back posts where the tilter balls could have been fitted. The balls, about one half a sphere, are shallow and are secured with leather thongs. These extend through holes drilled diagonally in the posts and are fastened with tacks where they emerge on the inside edges of the posts.

On the back of a letter addressed to Stephen Munsen of New Lebanon, there is a *Note from Betty to Br. Daniel Hawkins.* It is from Enfield, dated February 21, 1834, and states: *We have not any wool to make any more Chair Cushions this spring and shall not be able to get any more to send before the faul or spring after this.* Although Enfield was providing New Lebanon with either wool or woolen cushions, there is no evidence that the chairs in Enfield were cushioned. Leather, rush and cane were used in the seating of Enfield chairs.

Elkins records that one of his *pupils, a youth of fourteen years of*

Armed rocker, ca. 1840. Cane seat. (Collection of John Keith Russell)

Stereo view card, ca. 1880. This is one of a series of view cards taken of the Enfield Shaker Village. Chair is shown in this Victorian period room setting. (Courtesy of Hancock Shaker Village Inc., Pittsfield, Massachusetts)

age...bottome two chairs with flag; one with woven strands; covered eight or ten in leather;. Many of the chairs that today have cane seats show the impressions left by the firmly stretched rush which originally covered them.

The seat stretchers on cane seated chairs are usually oval or elliptical in shape with the ends turned round for tenons. Most were turned slightly oversize and flattened on the top and bottom to provide a flat surface for the cane. Others were shaped with moulding planes and then turned off center. The wider stretchers allowed additional wood for strength. The drilling of the many holes necessary for cane seating might overly weaken smaller round seat stretchers. The shaped stretchers also made it possible to recess the cane so that the finished seat was flush with the seat stretchers. The cane seating placed extra stress, tending to pull the tops of the stretchers towards one another. Fine nails inserted through the posts and into the seat stretchers prevent this from happening.

"... we felt a gift to rejoice with them in a lively dance—this was near the close of the Meeting, & after we had been sitting in Mother's great Chair ... "

October 26, 1834
Letter from Enfield, New Hampshire

Armless rocker, ca. 1840.

Most armless rockers from Enfield were intended for side chairs. The lower side stretchers are located close to the rockers and the back posts have sockets cut for tilters.

Photograph of Sister seated in Enfield rocker, date unknown. (Courtesy of Hancock Shaker Village, Inc., Pittsfield, Massachusetts.)

Bedroom, ca.1890-1920. Side chairs, ca.1840. Victorian bed possibly by the Cambridge and Folson Co. (From the Collection of the United Society of Shakers, Sabbathday Lake, Maine)

Young sisters making a rug, ca.1890-1920. Side chairs, ca.1840. Note the boots on the chair at the left. (From the Collection of the United Society of Shakers, Sabbathday Lake, Maine)

Detail of front post, side chair, ca.1840. These chairs are often numbered on the front posts or, occasionally, on the back slats. These numbers are probably room designations. Hervey Elkins describes the Great Stone Dwelling in his 1853 book and states: *"On either side are retiring rooms, all exactly twenty feet square, nine feet high, and of identical furniture and finish, rendering it difficult to determine, but by number, one room from another."* (Collection of Thomas and Jan Pavlovic)

Detail of tilter, side chair, ca.1840. (Private Collection)

Side chair, ca.1840. Classic Enfield tilter with slender proportions, overall balance, finely detailed graduation of back slats, and the perfected form of the simple pommel. Usually birch. Cane seat. (The Sherman Collection)

Work chair, ca.1840. Scribe marks on back posts correspond with those of a three slat side chair. These were disregarded to create a high seated two slat work chair. Rare and fine chair. Cane seat. Seat height— 21¼ inches. (Private Collection)

Armed rocker, ca.1840. Child's chair with typical Enfield pommels, slats, and front posts. The rockers and side scroll arm are not a common Enfield form. (Collection of John Keith Russell)

Lowback dining chair, ca.1840. Late Windsor chair derivation with wedge shaped crest rail and spindle back. Legs extended to produce a 19¼ inch seat height. Red paint. (Collection of John Keith Russell)

Though this chair is handmade, similar chairs were probably commercially manufactured outside the Shaker community at a later date for use in the dining rooms. Straight stretchers and machine tool marks distinguish the factory made chairs from those of the Shakers.

CANTERBURY, NEW HAMPSHIRE

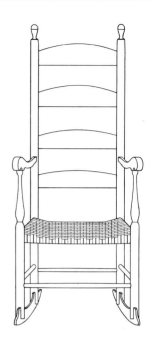

 The chairs from Canterbury are similar to those from Enfield, New Hampshire, but are more varied in detail and are not as delicate. Some of the features associated with Canterbury chairs appear to be unique.

While other Shaker chairs have seat stretchers mortised into the posts, two early rocking chairs from Canterbury have front posts mortised into corner blocks. This form is common on the Queen Anne style chair and is as close as a Shaker chair comes to being the product of the joiner's craft.

Two other features often distinguish Canterbury chairs from those of other Shaker communities. The bottom edges of the back slats of several chairs possess a downward or convex curve whereas the slats on most other Shaker chairs with the exception of those from South Union have straight bottom edges. Second, some pommels are adorned with a minute dome turning.

The pommel adorned with the additional dome turning represents one of three distinctive variations on the top of the back posts. The scribe mark at the widest diameter divides the pommel into two parts, the top being semi-spherical and the bottom gently tapering to the neck. This particular pommel is most often found on rocking chairs.

A second type of pommel found on some early Canterbury chairs is bulbous and symmetrical. The third, and most common, variation has scribe marks separating the short, rounded top from the more elongated, gently tapering bottom. While the top section of the pommel is rounded, it is not spherical as with the other two types. It is turned to a very slight point. Some of these pommels are difficult to distinguish from those on chairs from Enfield, New Hampshire.

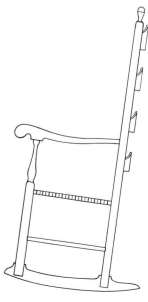

The posts have a very slight taper from the seat to the top. The back slats have a rounded bevel to the top edges, are usually graduated with the widest slat on top, and possess an arc across the top that is sometimes more pronounced that those on other Shaker chairs.

On armchairs, the front posts have a vase turning which is

gently shaped and tapered before forming a collar preceding the tenon. The arms are virtually identical to those on Enfield, New Hampshire, chairs.

The curvature of the top edges of the rockers between the posts is not as great as that on Enfield, New Hampshire, chairs. Neither is the concave/convex shape to the front and rear of the rockers. The rockers on Canterbury chairs have well defined segments which turn upwards at the posts. These are fitted into the posts and often extend on either side.

The form of the dining chair associated with Canterbury and Enfield, New Hampshire, reflects the influence of the Windsor chair. It has a solid plank seat and turned spindles in the back and is attributed to Micajah Tucker in 1834. Elder Henry Blinn records in his journal the following:

> *Instead of chairs at the dining table, the first Believers used long benches which accomodated some four or five persons each.*

Armless rocker, ca.1830. Rare low back rocker with corner blocks on front post. Very finely made. Dark varnish finish. (Courtesy of Hancock Shaker Village, Inc., Pittsfield, Massachusetts)

Armless rocker, ca.1830. Similar pommel to previous chair. The use of only four stretchers on rockers may be more common to Canterbury than to other communities. (Collection of John Keith Russell)

They were not convenient, especially, if one was obliged to leave the table before the others were ready. All were also under the necessity of sitting just as far from the table. Elder Br Micajah who was an excellent wood workman has now furnished the dining hall with chairs very much to the satisfaction of the family generally. At this date (1892) they are all in good repair.

As times changed so did tastes. The dining room was furnished anew in July of 1914 with the *Historical Record of Church Family, 1890-1930* reporting on the purchase:

Take out the table & chairs in the Family Dining Room. Have 7 tables 7 ft. x 3 ft. with opal glass tops made for us at a cost of $315.00. Also 56 Brown Leather Seat, Oak dining chairs costing $168 to take their places. They were bought (of) Hoitt and Company (a firm that is still in business in Manchester, New Hampshire).

Armless rocker, ca.1830. Small adult or large child's rocker. The pommel has a small dome shaped turning on the top. The back slats and their rounded top edges are less refined than on later Canterbury chairs. (Collection of DeGiorgis and Van Alstyne)

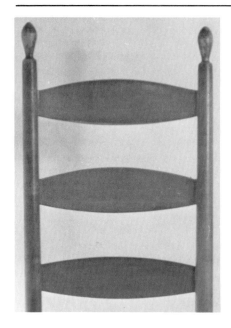

Side chair, ca. 1850. The convex shape on the top and bottom of the back slats is used on a small number of known Canterbury chairs. (Courtesy of New York State Museum, Albany, New York)

Side chair, ca.1850. The enlarged diameter turning where the seat stretchers meet the rear post is distinctive to this chair. It is one chairmaker's ingenious answer to the question of how to make a chair stronger at the point where it is naturally the weakest. (Collection of John Keith Russell)

Work chair, 1830. A stocky early work chair. Old rush seat. Seat height—25″. (Private Collection)

Work chair, ca.1850. An additional front stretcher was added as a foot rest. Seat height approx. 26″. (Courtesy of the Shaker Museum, Old Chatham, New York)

Armed rocker, ca.1850. The vase turning used on most Canterbury chairs is absent on this chair. Drop scroll armed rockers were made using three, four and five back slats. (Art Complex Museum of Duxbury)

"If you are privileged to sit in a rocking chair, you should endeavor to conform to the general custom of the company, but chairs without rockers should always rest their four posts on the floor."

Gentle Manners, 1899

Stereo view card, ca. 1890. View of dining room with holiday decorations and Windsor style low back dining chairs. (Courtesy of Hancock Shaker Village Inc., Pittsfield, Massachusetts)

Dining chair, ca. 1835. A Windsor influenced plank bottom chair. Boldly beveled seat. The thickness of the seat is not visible from the front. The legs are canted strongly toward the seat. The two outside back spindles have a square tenon to reduce the possibility of splitting the bent wedge shaped back rail. Pine and birch. This may be the style of dining chair attributed by Elder Henry Blinn to Brother Micajah Tucker. (Private Collection)

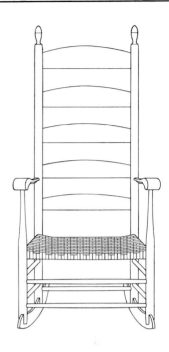

HARVARD, MASSACHUSETTS

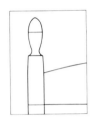

The provenance of existing chairs and references in existing account books and journals indicate that Harvard was a producer of chairs. It sold some chairs to the world as well as to neighboring Shaker communities and was the focal point for the development of a new style of chairs around the midpoint of the nineteenth century.

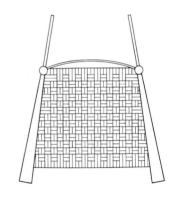

As early as 1828, the Harvard believers were making and selling chairs. The *Financial Accounts, 1826-1836* indicates that $1.00 was paid out for *bottoming chairs* on April 28, the same day that $6.00 was received for the sale of *1/2 Dozen Chairs.* The receipt of $1.00 for one chair is noted on February 13, 1832, and another $6.00 *by cash for Chairs* on December 26, 1834.

A Journal containing some of the most important events of the day kept for use & convenience of the Brethren of the church indicates an increase in chairmaking activities in the first few years of the 1840s. On February 3, 1841, *Elder Brother & Seth go to Ashburnham to see about chair stuff.*

Elder Brother (Thomas Hammond) *& Augustus* (probably Augustus Grosvenor) *are at work at the mill* on March 30, 1842, *turning chair stuff & sawing small sieve rims.* Shortly thereafter on May 13, *Elder Brother finished turning & boring chair stuff today for the present...*

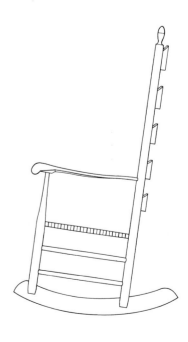

A reference from January 21 of the following year indicates that not all these chairs were immediately finished: *Dana White & Elisha Myrick are and have been for some days past seating chairs for the present. They have seated in all this winter 73 chairs.* A notation on January 14, 1845, notes that Brother Elisha was again seating chairs.

An account of chairs made in this family in the years 1841 and 1842 is listed on January 28, 1843. It states that Elder Brother Thomas Hammond was *foreman in making the chairs. Amount including all sizes 339.* The frames were finished on August 23, 1842, and *There was put to the office 83 common, 3 Rocking chairs with arms, and 6 small ones, 92 in all.* There *was carried to the office for sale 1 dozen frames (common) and 1 dozen small frames. Making in all carried to the office 116 chairs. To the Ministry 12 common and 2 small ones, to the 2nd family 7 seated chairs, to North Enfield 1 seated chair, to Shirley 1 small frame.* Account references to chairmaking during the decade of the 1840s conclude with a notation on May 4, 1849, of *cash for Rocking chairs-$4.37.*

These chairs by Elder Brother Thomas and company may be those recognized today as the typical Harvard chair. Tall and majestic, the chair has well-turned, elongated pommels that continue in an unbroken curve from the tops to the sharp shoulders. Single scribe marks divide the pommels at their center points.

The back posts are usually straight, although a few exhibit a slight bend beginning at the seat. The scribe marks on the posts distinguish Harvard chairs from those of other communities. While there are sometimes no scribe marks for the placement of the slats, the usual method is the use of a single mark to indicate the lower edge of each slat. Usually, there is another scribe mark for the seat stretchers and, occasionally, another just above the seat stretchers. On rocking chairs single scribe marks appear near the bottom of the rear posts to indicate the depth of the rockers. The marks do not appear on the front posts.

The broad back slats have a gentle arc, are often graduated, and possess a rounded bevel on their top front edges. Sometimes only the top slat has the rounded bevel.

The chairs seated with cane have brads inserted through the posts into the seat stretchers. These are usually covered with wood filler and are necessary to prevent the cane from twisting the seat stretchers.

The front posts have a smooth convex taper between the seat and the arms, into which the posts are mortised. The arms are a variation of the drop scroll style, but have a distinctive chamfering on the underside of the handhold that separates them from chairs produced at Alfred, as well as those of the world commonly called "The Boston Rocker."

The rockers on Harvard chairs have a continuous arc on the top that extends from the curved front to the terminating curve at the back. These are fastened to the posts by the use of rivets and burrs.

The tilters are approximately half of a sphere, making them noticeably different than those of most other communities. Leather thongs which secure the tilters extend straight up through holes drilled in the center of the posts to the stretcher holes. Additional holes are drilled from inside the back posts to the same stretcher holes, allowing the thongs to extend to the exterior of the posts. The thongs are usually fastened with two tacks.

Some Harvard chairs appear to have been manufactured at a later date, as factory methods of production are apparent. The side stretchers which still show machine tool marks are not tapered as they approach the posts. The tenons, instead of having been turned on the lathe, were cut with a chucking head.

Near the end of 1852, the construction of the South Family of

Harvard was finished. The following year the office at the Church Family was completed. Throughout 1853 and 1854, numerous buildings were erected which may have created the need for additional chairs. A series of letters between Elder Grove Blanchard of Harvard and members from the ministry that guided the communities of Hancock and Enfield, Connecticut, indicates the care and interest invested in changing the design of the chairs.

Enfield, Aug. 15th, 1853

Beloved Ministry,

Your very acceptable letter bearing date of Aug. 8th, 1852 is at hand and ordinary promptness would seem to demand an earlier reply; but as its "particular objective" is in regard to Chairs - rather an easy sort of a subject - it may yet be in season.

Elder Harvey & others are all pleased with the preliminary steps you have taken in order to secure at the outset a proper pattern of that necessary & convenient article of household furniture. And should circumstances operate favorably you may consider it as pretty much settled for some one or ones to meet you at Lovely Vineyard and pass upon the comelings of the improved Pattern. Elder Grove does not think it necessary for any one from these parts to repair to the Manufactory, but would prefer to settle all matters at your place. It may, therefore, be as well to have said pattern properly fashioned and in readings at Lovely Vineyard as soon as convenient for reasons which will more fully appear hereafter.

Ministry
City of Union

Watch-Hill, Westerly (Rhode Island),
Aug. 25, 1853

Brother Elder Grove,

When we left home, there was talk of our returning by way of Harvard, and to look at that Chair, concerning which you wrote. But at present there is little or no prospect of returning that way. So now what shall be done about this Chair Business. There is one way which was talked of, before we left home, in case we should not return by way of Harvard. If you could consistantly leave home for a few days to take the Sample Chair when done and come to Enfield, where we can all look at it and suggest sutch alterations as may appear adviseable &, &. Now I know this is asking too much, but we will guarantee, that as far as primary matters are concerned, it shall cost you nothing.

(No signature)

City of Union, Aug. 31, 1853

Respecting the Chair business, we unite with you in having a sample (as soon as consistant) forwarded to Shaker Village, & have them inspected at Holy Mount, as it appears to be a matter of considerable consequence to get something started about right & something which can be owned and blessed at the fountain head, seeing that we are agoing to vary from the old standard among believers.

So now when ever you send on the samples, we will endeavor to have them forwarded to Holy Mount for examination & return you an answer accordingly. Pleas write at the time you send the chairs & suggest such alter-ations as you may think would be an improvement & if any these should be.

As to Balls in the back posts, I have heard nothing particular said, but suppose Believers generally will want them as they prevent maring the floor etc. But most likely, we shall have that part to do our selves. But the hind posts will have to be turned suitable for the purpose. When you write pleas name what the calculations are respecting Balls & whither you are expecting to have any.

.......*In Union,*
Grove

(Undated)

Kind & dearest friend, Elder Grove.
..... *I mentioned the matter to the Ministry at Holy Mount respecting the Chairs etc. & that we expected a sample sent on soon. Elder Amos said he should like well to see one.*

Most likely geting these chairs may cause a change in the fashion of Chairs among Believers which will be no harm if there can be any alternate for the better.

I hope when you send on the sample chairs you will be particular in stating your views as to any alterations etc. which you may think advisable or that may be an improvement.

(Unsigned)

West Pittsfield, December 2nd '53
Beloved Elder Grove,
This will inform you that we expect to go to Enfield on Tuesday the 6th . . . where we shall probably stay, as much as four weeks and should those sample chairs be made within that time we shall like to have them sent to Enfield or rather to Springfield.

The South family are about moving into their new house, this week & begin to feel in somthing of a hurry about some new chairs.

Now Kind Elder, should the chairs be ready in the course of 2 or 3 weeks, and you should feel as tho you could spare time & come to Enfield when the chairs come along, we should like it right well, you may be sure; in this way we can all look at the chairs and talk & contrive & suggest alterations if there are any needed, &c. And we will guarantee that the old contract shall stand good, as to expenses &c. And should it be inconsistent for you to come in person, perhaps you may send a Deputy.

The Ministry at Holy Mount feel considerable interest in the new fashioned chairs & they hope there may be somthing got up about right which will do for believers to pattern after, & will be an improvement as to chairs.

As there are considerable of a quantity like to be wanted to begin with, it is of some consequence to start as near right as possible. There will probably be between one & two hundred wanted at Enfield.

We shall like to receive a few lines from you soon after we get to Enfield stating about the Chairs &c. and what the probability is respecting some one from your City taking a trip to Enfield at the time the Chairs come on. It will give a much better opportunity for examination & consultation if you could just step out to Old Enfield than what it would for one of us to come to your place; as the chairs can be inspected at your place before they are sent on.

But we will confide in your judgment & wisdom in the matter, trusting that all will be done right...

In Union, Grove

The journal of Thomas Damon of Hancock notes that Elder Grove Blanchard and Elder Wm. Leonard of Harvard visited Enfield, Connecticut, on January 2, 1854, *with a new style of chair which it was proposed to introduce among Believers.* Three days later, they went to New Lebanon with the sample chairs and then to Hancock. The entry for January 11 records that *the Rocking chair is condemned except for the sick and the small chair admitted with some modification.*

The following week, the Harvard journals mention that Elder Grove went *to Ashburnham about chair.* This town was well known for its chairmaking factories, a trade that started there as early as 1805 and employed more than 200 men in one shop in 1870. *A feature of the business at this time,* records the town history, *was the sale of turned stock in the lower towns and, in fact, ... few ... were engaged in the manufacture of finished chairs.* Late in the century, the annual production of chairs in Ashburnham reached 360,000. *We should suppose that at the rate chairs are made at the Factory you speak of, the world would soon be furnished,* wrote Jefferson White from Enfield, Connecticut, to Elder Grove on January 25, 1854. Within the month, *Augustus & Elder Harvey* (went from Harvard) *to Ashburnham about chairs. . .*

Letters from this period show that the Shakers considered purchasing chairs or chair parts from these world's factories. Although documentation is not available to prove or disprove specific purchases by the Harvard community, they may have bought a quantity of chairs.

Diary account. Fine documentation of chairs made by Brother Thomas Hammond during the 1840s. (Courtesy of the Fruitlands Museums, Harvard, Massachusetts)

Detail of riveted rocker extensions. (Private Collection)

worked at it for some time past.

An account of Chairs made in this Family in the years 1841 and 42 Elder Brother Thomas Hammond foreman in makeing the Chairs. Amount including all Sizes 339. Finished the frames August 23 1842. There was put to the Office 83 Common 3 Rocking chairs with arms, and 6 small ones 92 in all

January 1843

28 The account of Chairs continued. Was carried to the Office for Sale 1 dozen frames (Common) and 1 dozen Small frames making in all carried to the Office 116 chaires. To the Ministry 12 Common and 2 Small ones. To the 2d family 7 Seated chaires. To North Enfield 1 Seated chair To Shirley 1 small frame.

Armless rocker, ca. 1840. Back slats, uniformly graduated. On four or five slat rockers, only the top slat has a rounded edge; the others are slightly beveled. (Courtesy of the Fruitlands Museums, Harvard, Massachusetts)

Detail of back slat and pommel typical of Harvard chairs. Top front edge of slat usually rounded. A single scribe line, located at the bottom, marks the location of the slat. (Courtesy of the Fruitlands Museums, Harvard, Massachusetts)

Detail of rocker and front post. Rivets were commonly used to fasten rocker blades to posts on Harvard chairs. This detail, rarely used on other Shaker chairs, is helpful in identifying chairs from Harvard. (Courtesy of the Fruitlands Museums, Harvard, Massachusetts)

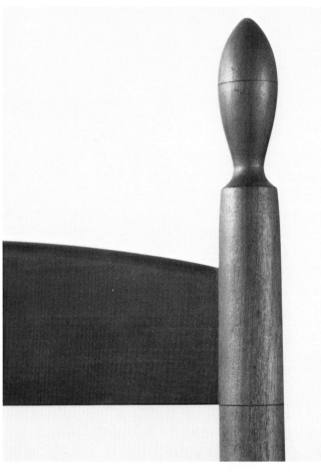

Armed rocker, ca.1840. Distinctly and finely shaped arms. Old green paint. Old splint seat. (Collection of Robert and Kathleen Booth, Photograph by Karl Ott)

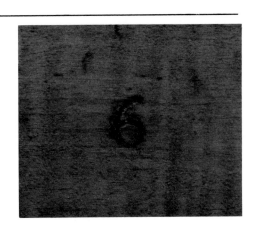

The photographs that follow show a progression of design in Harvard side chairs. Ca.1820. The earliest chair has very heavy posts and an awkward pommel design. (Courtesy of the Hancock Shaker Village, Inc., Pittsfield, Massachusetts)

Ca.1830. Much lighter though not yet very refined. (Courtesy of the Hancock Shaker Village, Inc., Pittsfield, Massachusetts)

Ca.1840-50. Refined and finely detailed. Optimum dimensions for a fine chair. Pleasant pommels and balanced back slats. (Probably 1 inch missing from posts.) (Courtesy of the Hancock Shaker Village, Inc., Pittsfield, Massachusetts)

Ca.1860-80. Awkward compared to other Harvard chairs. Unusual third side stretcher. Many details including tool marks and tenons on stretchers indicate commercial manufacture. This might be one of the "factory" chairs discussed in the letters in the text of this chapter. (Courtesy of the Fruitlands Museums, Harvard, Massachusetts)

Side chairs, ca.1840-50. Figured maple.
Unusually high seats—18 inches. Tilters.
(Collection of Robert and Katharine Booth.
Photograph by Karl Ott)

Armless rocker, ca.1850. Small child's size. Several two slat rockers and side chairs exist. Width of the Harvard slats is obvious on a small chair. (Courtesy of the Fruitlands Museums, Harvard, Massachusetts)

Armless rocker, ca.1850. Unusual number of stretchers on this small adult rocker. (Courtesy of the Fruitlands Museums, Harvard, Massachusetts)

Armless rocker, ca.1840-50. Figured wood. (Courtesy of the Fruitlands Museums, Harvard, Massachusetts)

Armless rocker, ca.1840-50. The ultimate in the armless rockers. Extremely fine proportions. Curly maple. (Private Collection)

(Opposite) **Armed rocker, ca.1820.** Figured maple. (Collection of John Keith Russell)

ENFIELD, CONNECTICUT

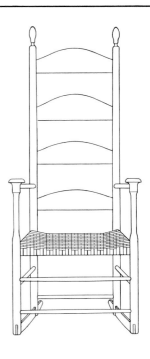

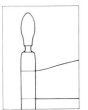

There are numerous chairs that have a provenance connecting them to the Enfield, Connecticut, community. This connection is supported by a fine historical photograph of Sister Emily Copley and four young women seated in typical Enfield chairs.

In the early days of the Shaker faith, a close relationship existed between Enfield and Watervliet, New York. Father Joseph Meacham, the organizational genius of the United Society of Believers, also was the founder of the Connecticut community. This may be why the chairs of Enfield are close in design to those of Watervliet.

Rocking chairs from the first quarter of the nineteenth century from Enfield reflect a basic simplicity. The usually tall and dignified backs receive slightly rounded crescent shaped arms. These extend to the minimally shaped front posts where they are tenoned beneath the circular mushroom-shaped handholds.

The pommels are elongated ovals in which a slight concave indentation occurs about two-thirds of the way down. A sharp edge is then formed where the bottom of this collar meets the bold concave turning that defines the neck. The tops of the pommels on Enfield chairs are more flattened than those from Watervliet.

The back posts are straight and receive slats that are graduated in contour as well as in height. This graduation is obtained by an increase in the height at the center of the slats without a corresponding increase in height where they are tenoned into the posts. A strong flat chamfer on the top front edges of the slats adds an element of refinement.

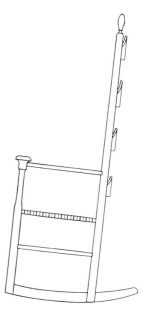

The front posts have no decorative turnings but shallow indentations above the seat which lead to short portions the same diameter as the sections below the seat. Mushroom-shaped handholds are turned on top of the front posts. This form requires that the wood from which the posts were turned be about three inches in diameter. The chairmaker had to remove well over half of the bulk of the wood to form posts about 1½ inches in diameter.

The rockers are thin blades, almost uniform in height from front to back, and do not extend beyond the front posts.

Several children's chairs from Enfield have greatly elongated pommels with the oval shape continuing in an uninterrupted line into the lengthy collars. The slats do not have the strong contour that is seen on the earlier adult's chairs; nor are the slats as heavily chamfered along the top front edges.

A letter addressed to Elder Grove Blanchard at Harvard by Jefferson White at Enfield is the primary document concerning the chairs at Enfield and implies a decline of chairmaking in that community by the middle of the nineteenth century. This letter accompanies the series of letters printed in the Harvard chapter of this book and concerns Harvard's involvement in the production and distribution of a *new style* of chair.

> *City of Union, January 25th, 1854*
>
> *Beloved Elder Grove,*
>
> *Your kind favor of the 21st is safe at hand. We all were pleased to learn that you had a prosperous trip & arrived safe at home. We all make you thrice welcome to the little we did for you while here, would that you could have tarried longer with us. But we feel thankful for the short privilege that we had with you & Elder William.*
>
> *As to the Chairs, we have concluded to have no Birdseye maple for the slats, as it will cost considerable more. So please have all the chairs made as per sample chair with variations mentioned by you. We were not much surprised as to the Rocking chairs knowing that there would be danger in having to many of these. We shall want the chairs as soon as ready. We have been highly pleased that Elder Grove has had some agency in the Cloth & chair business. For by this means have had the privilege to see you here & to hear from you by letter. It seemed to work curious about the Cloth, we probably wrote the same day you did & asked for 200 yards more of cloth, we have received the bill of cloth 829 3/4 yds at 10 1/4 per yd. $84.97 credit to Br Janas.*
>
> *We think the chairs may be matted so as to come safe. We supposed they will be all finished off ready (for use) ere they are sent to us, which is what we should chuse. We wish to have the chairs sent to us at Springfield Mass. It will save expense & perhaps save some overhauling of them. We hope they may be put in a Car which will come into Springfield. ...*
>
> *We have our kind friends at Harvard & we always feel well pleased when we can get a letter from them, especially from such a (good) and kind friend as our Elder Grove is whom we love in the truth. We sometimes wish we could have two Elder Grove, the one named above as well as the other. But that is asking too much.*
>
> *We suppose that at the rate chairs are made at the Factory you speak of, the world would soon be furnished ...*

Side chairs, ca.1840. Two fine figured maple child's chairs. Exquisite form and proportions often difficult to find in small chairs. Tilters. (Private Collection. Photograph by Richard P. Meyer)

X-ray of pommel. Metal rod inserted into a hole drilled about 5 inches into the top of the post to strengthen the narrow neck of the pommel. (Private Collection)

X-ray of tilter in socket. (Private Collection)

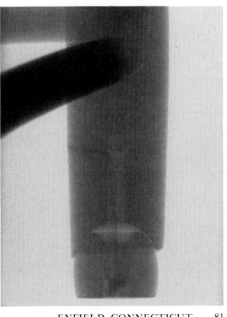

Armed rocker, ca.1810. Unusual proportions. Mushroom post rockers are usually much taller and have four slats. (The Stokes Collection)

Armed rocker, ca.1820. Very fine mushroom post rocker of excellent proportions. Exquisite graduation of back slats. (Douglas and Cornelia Hamel)

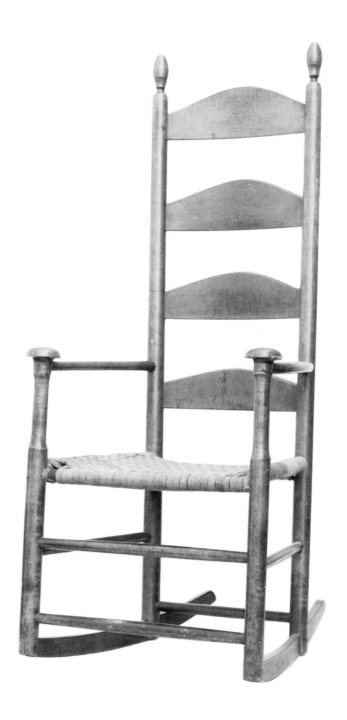

(Opposite) **Armed rocker, ca.1830. Alfred.**
Side scroll arms with handhold located in
front of front post. Simple arm supports
and rocker blades. Yellow paint. (Collection
of Thomas and Jan Pavlovic)

ALFRED AND SABBATHDAY LAKE, MAINE

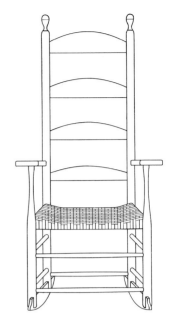

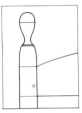

Alfred and Sabbathday Lake chair makers generally adhered to the simple slat back style chair used throughout the United Society of Believers even though they were the eastern communities located the greatest distance from the Central Ministry. The attribution of Maine Shaker chairs to either Alfred or Sabbathday Lake is difficult because of the close relationship of these two communities.

Journals note that when leaders and members moved between communities their personal belongings were often moved with them. Thus, chairs which might have been at Sabbathday Lake prior to the Alfred closing, might not necessarily have been made at Sabbathday Lake. This intermingling of the furnishings of the two communities became even greater when truckloads of property were transported to Sabbathday Lake from Alfred when it closed in 1931.

The *No. 1 Ledger Book* from Alfred indicates chairs were made in that community at an early date. Three chairs were *sold to Able Hamilton* for $1.38 on December 20, 1834. A notation in *Book 2* shows 63 cents received for one chair. Over the years, about thirty chairs are listed as sold from the Alfred community along with other furniture including a *candel stand,* tables, chests and numerous beds. An 1829 entry pertains to mending chairs. There is no further known reference to chairs until the turn of the century. As noted in the New Lebanon chapter of this book, in 1909, Elder Henry Green from Alfred sold chairs manufactured at New Lebanon on his regular sales routes to the outside world.

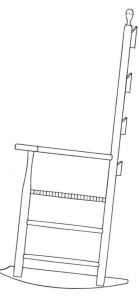

Chairs made in the Maine communities more closely approximate the New England slat back chair than those from any of the other communities. This is especially true of the chairs from Sabbathday Lake which are stockier than most Shaker chairs. The pommels on Maine chairs are more bulbous than on those from other Shaker communities except for Pleasant Hill whose turnings are similar to those from Sabbathday Lake.

Scribe marks often adorn the pommels of Alfred chairs. Double or triple marks symmetrically placed around the midpoint are traits that help to establish that they were made in Alfred. The base of the bulbous pommels narrows to a neck before enlarging to a small ridge that forms the shoulder on top of the back posts.

The back posts of the Alfred side chair are distinctive in that they are bent noticeably backward just above the scribe marks that indicate the placement of the seat. This abrupt bend is made in just four or five inches of the posts.

Scribe marks on the posts locate graduated back slats with the top one secured in the posts by single or double pins extending completely through the posts. Occasionally the second slat from the top is also pinned. The top front edge of the bent slats are usually rounded.

The stretchers are tapered in a continually increasing diameter towards well defined scribe marks adorning the center points of the stretchers. This feature which imitates the "bamboo" turnings on many Windsor chairs is not seen on chairs from other Shaker communities.

Armed rockers from Alfred have variations of the drop scroll and the side scroll arm. These receive the front post tenons well behind the bulk of the handhold. The Alfred drop scroll arm is less intricately detailed than those on Harvard chairs. It is similar to the arm common to "Boston" rockers popularized by many of the world's manufacturers in the last half of the nineteenth century. The arm is supported by the front post turned to very slender size above the seat stretchers. The top front edges of the obviously graduated back slats are finished with a slight bevel. The top slat is fastened into the posts with two pegs; the second slat is secured with only one. The rockers are abruptly cut on both ends and are held to the post with wood pegs.

A second style of armed rocker is distinguished by its arms. Although the standard description of the side scroll arm is applicable, this chair is quite different from those made at New Lebanon. The front posts are tenoned into the arms behind the scroll, a form similar to a rocker made at Pleasant Hill.

One style of arm is uniform in thickness between the posts and is similar to the arms on chairs from New Lebanon and Pleasant Hill. Another style decreases in thickness from the front to the back and exhibits severe chamfering from the outside edges to the posts on the underside of the hand holds. Unlike the arms on most New Lebanon chairs the edges are only slightly rounded. The arm supports between the seat and the arms are the simplest of all Shaker chairs. The continuous concave taper is broken only by the smooth collar before it is tenoned into the arm.

The rocker blades are slotted into the bottoms of the posts and are much broader where they rest on the floor than near the ends where they are secured into the posts by pegs.

The primary seating materials of the Maine communities were leather, supplied by the Alfred community tannery, splint and woven tapes. As late as 1875, Elder Henry Green made two-harness looms for weaving tape, narrow braid, and straw. The brilliant red and blue tapes that appear on many of the remaining Alfred chairs might have been produced on these looms.

ELDRESS PRUDENCE STICKNEY
OF THE SABBATHDAY LAKE SHAKERS

Side chair, ca.1810-40. Sabbathday Lake. Early, primitive chair. (From the Collection of the United Society of Shakers, Sabbathday Lake, Maine)

Side chair, ca.1820. Sabbathday Lake. Adapted as work chair. Boards added to raise seat height for use at a loom. (From the Collection of the United Society of Shakers, Sabbathday Lake, Maine)

Armless rocker, ca.1880. Sabbathday Lake. Several child's rockers have been attributed to Brother William Dumont. All have heavy construction, short simple rockers and short backs with two or three slats. (From the Collection of the United Society of Shakers, Sabbathday Lake, Maine)

Brother William Dumont. 1851-1930. (Courtesy of the Shaker Library, The United Society of Shakers, Sabbathday Lake, Maine)

Sisters making fancy goods at Alfred. Note the bent back posts of the ca.1840 Alfred chairs. (Courtesy of the Shaker Library, The United Society of Shakers, Sabbathday Lake, Maine)

Side chair, ca.1840. Alfred. Bent back posts, beveled and graduated slats with top slat pinned. Taper above seat on front posts. Scribe line on pommels. Influence of Windsor bamboo chairs in the swell and central line on stretchers. Hand woven tape. (From the Collection of the United Society of Shakers, Sabbathday Lake, Maine)

Armed rocker, ca.1840. Alfred. Small, low seated chair. Side scroll arms and slender, simple front posts. Arms heavily chamfered on the bottom edges. (From the Collection of the United Society of Shakers, Sabbathday Lake, Maine)

Armed rocker, ca.1830. Alfred. Note the rounded edge on the underside of the arms. Primitive rockers on an otherwise refined chair. (From the Collection of the United Society of Shakers, Sabbathday Lake, Maine)

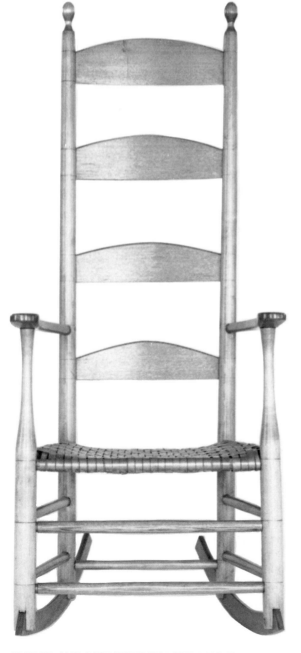

Armed rocker, ca. 1840. Alfred. Heavily scribed short pommels. Front scroll arms are similar to the "Boston rockers" of the world. Rockers are different from those on other Alfred chairs. (From the Collection of the United Society of Shakers, Sabbathday Lake, Maine)

Eldress Mary Walker on porch, ca. 1910. Alfred. Wood Photo Co. (Courtesy of the Shaker Library, the United Society of Shakers. Sabbathday Lake, Maine)

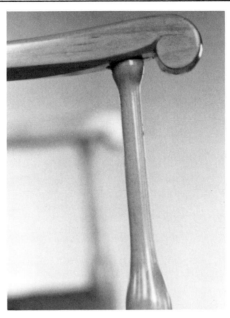

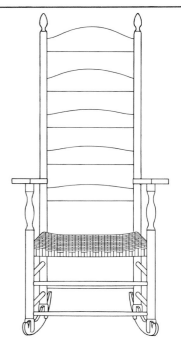

NORTH UNION, UNION VILLAGE, WATERVLIET, AND WHITEWATER, OHIO

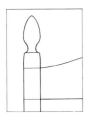

Chairs produced in the four Shaker communities of North Union, Union Village, Watervliet, and Whitewater are considered together in this section under the single heading of Ohio. Inaccuracies in oral attributions are bound to have occurred in the seventy-year interval between the closing of these communities and the present day. Adding to the potential for confusion was the movement of people and properties to Union Village when the other three communities closed. For example, chairs of the style that have long been associated with North Union have been found in the area near Whitewater and Union Village, the new homes of the members of North Union when their village closed in 1889.

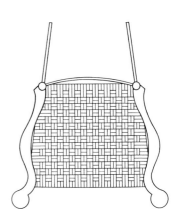

Union Village was the first and last Shaker community in Ohio, existing from 1804 to 1912. It was in this community that the foremost Shaker in Ohio, Brother Richard McNemar, pursued his skills as a craftsman. From Union Village came the journal and financial accounts in which references to the making of chairs are found. Therefore, most of the information and examples of Ohio Shaker chairs come from this community.

Although the *Financial Accounts of the Shaker Community in the Miami Valley, Ohio* begin in 1807, it is not until May 29, 1813, that an entry is found pertaining to chairs: *Nathan received $5.25 dollars for chairs.* On August 10 of the same year, *Rec'd of Nathaniel Murphy for chairs, 1.25.* One month later a notation was made stating, *Rec'd by the hand of Richard for a set of chairs sold to Isaac Morris senior, $5.25.* The same amount was received *of Richard for one set of chairs* on October 7 and November 6 while $11 was entered on November 30.

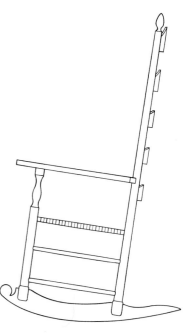

Brother Richard McNemar had been the minister of the largest Presbyterian church in southern Ohio before becoming one of the first converts to the Shaker faith at Union Village. He was known as a weaver, bookbinder, printer, author, preacher, and songwriter. In his notes on the diaries of Brother Richard, the Ohio historian J.P. McLean credits the Shaker leader with 1,403 chairs before May, 1821.

The *Whole number since Nov. 15, 1813, til Dec. 1817* was 757 in addition to *Big wheels—200, Little wheels—20, Reels—20, spools, Fliers, wheels & repairs without count.* Included in these numbers were *3 chair frames . . . 1.50* on January 14, 1814, and *one set of blue chairs* for $5.50 to a woman on March 7 of the same year. Chairs were also sold to a Samuel Alexander and a Peter Winton.

Brother Richard was both a prodigious chairmaker and an active leader in the faith. He was involved in the effort to establish other Shaker communities in Ohio at Darby Plains, Eagle Creek, North Union and Whitewater during the early 1820s, but by 1825 he was back in Union Village at his manual trade. On February 15 of that year he *fixed up a lathe for chairmaking.* Four days later he *finished two chair frames.* On February 14, 1828, six chairs were sold at 62½¢ to Ebenezer Anderson but shortly thereafter Brother Richard returned to his leadership role when he moved to Watervliet, Ohio, until the end of 1835 at which time he returned to Union Village. In a letter to *Much Esteemed Br. Ruffus* (Bishop) on October 28, 1837, Elder Richard wrote: *Hence I have not so unreservedly devoted my time to the loom & turning lathe as to spend no part in the museum or book department.*

In 1836 Elder Richard was joined by another chairmaker. The *Records of the Church at Watervliet, N.Y.* report on March 17 of that year that *Necessity seems to require some person to go to the west to stand first in care at Union Village, Ohio. Accordingly, it is felt to be best by the Ministry for Freegift Wells, the second elder in the chh* (Church) *at Watervliet to go home with Elder Matthew as soon as circumstances will permit and stand as first in care at Union Village.* Brother Freegift left for Ohio on April 12.

On June 1, 1837, Elder Freegift's journals record that he was *engaged in bottoming chairs with list.* This notation indicates the early use of listing, or tapes, for chair seats at Union Village.

The Ministry returned from Whitewater this evening, Elder Freegift records in his journal on September 28, 1837. *Daniel Searing came with them after a lot of chairs & to see a part of a lathe from the East.* Journal entries show Elder Freegift pursuing the chairmaking trade in Ohio:

July 9, 1839—F. has been plaining out chair posts.

July 10—F. has rough turned a parcel of rounds for chair backs.

July 31—F. gets along very slow with the chairs. He has just got the 4 seats frames pinned together.

With the movement of craftsmen, the Shaker style was transmitted from one community to another.

One style of Ohio Shaker chair closely resembles that of chairs in other Shaker communities. It has finely turned elliptical pommels and arched back slats with the top front edges of the slats rounded. Mortised into the back posts, the slats are fastened with pegs usually

driven from the back. The slats are most often graduated in width, with the narrowest starting at the bottom and the widest at the top.

The second style of Ohio Shaker chair exhibits marked regional influence. This style of chair has the back posts flattened on the front beginning below the lowest slat on side chairs or just above the arm on armchairs. The flattened front edges terminate in a chamfer or curve that meets the back edge of the posts. These chairs have slats that are flat on the top edges and notched at the upper corners before entering the back posts. Usually the depth of notching decreases progressively from the top slat to the lowest slat. Chairs from Watervliet, however, often have only the top slat notched, and held in place in the posts by two small brads in each slat. The brads enter into the posts from the front.

This style of chair with notched back slats and with or without turned pommels are common in southwest Ohio during this period

Side chair, ca.1840. Union Village. Corner notched graduated back slats secured into posts with two brads from the front. Rear post flattened on the front. Front post stamped "7." Diameter of posts reduces rapidly below bottom stretchers. (Warren County Historical Society)

of Shaker chairmaking. It is not clear whether the Shakers influenced local craftsmen or vice versa.

The posts on side chairs often reach their greatest diameter about two inches above the floor, below which they show a marked concave reduction. From this thickest point, the posts taper gradually upwards to their tops. On rocking chairs, the base of the posts often have an enlarged turning for the reception of the rockers. On armchairs, the front posts have vase-shaped turnings between the seat and the arms before the transition to an enlarged diameter upon which the arms rest.

Two styles of arms adorn most Ohio Shaker chairs. One is a flat arm with a side scroll pattern similar to that on chairs from New

Lebanon, Pleasant Hill, and other communities. The other is a flat cyma or S-curve arm which is distinctive to Union Village.

Rocking chairs have thin, flat rockers inserted into a slot in the posts. These are secured in place by wooden pegs. The top edges of the rockers are often shaped upward where they meet the posts and have a finely shaped scrolled front.

Although the journal of Amy Slaters from Union Village records on November 3, 1848, that she was *weaving tape, dying cloth madder red,* this type of seating material is absent on surviving examples of chairs from that community. Splint and leather were the dominant materials used, the latter being a product of Union Village's extensive tannery business.

North Union purchased *Canterbury tape* for $9.00 on October 16, 1851, but sold some to Union Village for $10.37 in December, 1853. They were weaving tapes of all widths in 1856. In April of that year, they received $35.06 for seating chairs and an additional $7.75 in July. They sold four *Gentlemen's Cushions* at 3¢ each on August 24, 1855. The community of Watervliet paid $2.19 on January 1, 1857, *For timber to bottom chairs.*

In addition to the corner-notched slats and the S-shaped arms, Ohio Shaker chairs can often be distinguished by their color. A red stain was used on dining chairs, and a cantaloupe orange decorated most of the other chairs from the southwest Ohio communities. This color was often accented with blue and yellow on the arms or similar colors on the rockers.

Side chair, ca.1840. Slightly arched slats similar to those on New Lebanon chairs. Concave taper at base of posts. Orange paint. (Murphy Collection)

Side chair, ca.1830. Arched slats with beveled top edges. "5" stamped on top of left post. Orange paint. (Mr. and Mrs. Jack Rhodus)

Work chair, ca.1840. Slats made of two pieces of wood glued together horizontally. Top of slats sharply beveled. Slats pinned from back. Scribe mark centered vertically on front of slats. The posts are tapered over nearly their full length. The largest diameter is just below the bottom stretchers where it is sharply tapered to the bottom. (Murphy Collection)

Side chair, ca.1840. Watervliet. Corner-notched top slat secured with brads from the front. Additional scribe mark on posts indicated depth of the notch on the top slat. Donut turning at top of front posts. (Mr. and Mrs. Jack Rhodus)

Dining chair, ca. 1830. Union Village. Rear posts planned flat above the seat. Two corner notched slats secured with brads. Scribe marks are not used to locate the back slats or stretchers. (Mr. and Mrs. Jack Rhodus)

Chair on wheels, ca. 1830. Front surface of rear post planned flat. Two corner notched slats secured with wood pins. Enlarged turning at base of posts. Wood wheels secured with large pegs. (The Jones Collection, Golden Lamb Inn)

Side chair, ca.1840. Union Village. Corner notched graduated back slats secured into posts with two brads from the front. Rear posts flattened on the front. Front post stamped "16." Diameter of posts reduces rapidly below bottom stretchers. (Warren County Historical Society)

Armed rocker, ca.1840. S-curve arms. Back slats notched in descending depth with the bottom slat not corner notched. Unusual vase turning on front post. (Private Collection)

Armed rocker, ca. 1830. Union Village. S-curve arms. Enlarged turning at base of posts. Boldly scrolled rocker blades pegged to posts. (Warren County Historical Society. Photograph courtesy of Columbus Museum of Art)

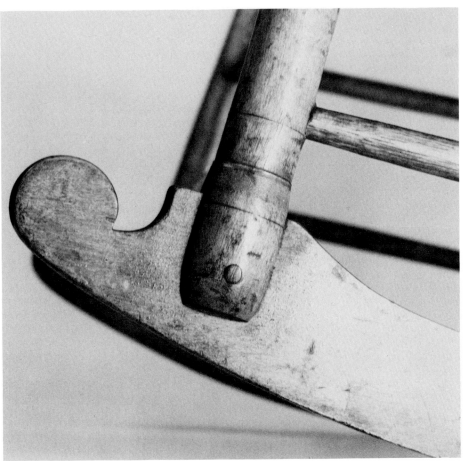

PLEASANT HILL, KENTUCKY

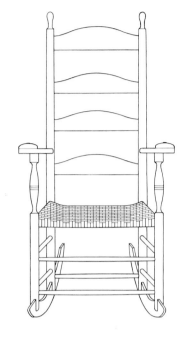

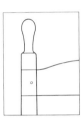An early account book notes *chairs bottomed & painted—$2.50* on October 12, 1817, but most of the resource material relating to chairmaking at Pleasant Hill is contained in a journal from the middle of the nineteenth century. *A Temporal Journal Kept by order of the Deacon of the East House... Book B* begins on January 1, 1843, and includes *an account of Family work, concerns and accomodations; Produce for sale; Boughten Articles; and Brethren's shoes.* This document names Brother Francis Monfort as a primary chairmaker, whose work furnished many of the families. The following are excerpts from that journal:

January 10, 1843	*2 Chair frames, one an arm chair, for East Family by F.M.*
	4 Common chair frames for Centre Family by F. Monfort
January 12, 1843	*1 Arm chair for East Family by F. Monfort*
	Also turned 4 bedstead legs
December 10, 1844	*A Stools chair for Joseph, made by Francis*
January 16, 1845	*Three sweating chairs, one for each Family, and a common chair for Centre Family, made by F. Monfort*
January 21, 1845	*2 little chairs for home made by F. Monfort*
December 22, 1846	*Francis Monfort has made 4 chairs for the Office & one for sale, 2 arm chairs for the Centre Family, 26 chairs for the East Family, 3 reels repaired for the Centre Family, one turning lathe for himself, a bedstead and wheel for the East Family...*
February 9, 1847	*7 Chairs for the Centre Family, made by F. Monfort*
December 5, 1848	*F. Monfort has made 2 chairs, 2 Ginnies ...for the Centre Family; A little table, 2 little chairs, 3 arm chairs...for the East Family;... One little chair for the Office...*

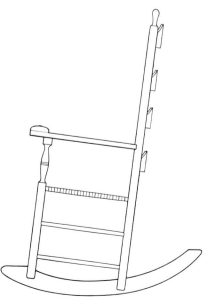

besides about 500 sundry small articles and mending...

After this date, it is clear that the journal records year-end summaries which attribute to Brother Francis the following:

1850　*...for the Center Fam....1 sewing stools, 1 gate for the garden, 1 jointer for himself...For the West Family 1 arm chair...*

1852　*...for the Center Family 8 common chairs, 2 arm chairs ...For the East House 8 common chairs...and 584 basket ribs. For the West Family 1 little chairs, 12 common chairs...*

1853　*...for the Center Family...1 arm chair, 1 little chair... For the East Family, a turning lathe set up in the brick shop east room below, 1 Cupboard for cellar...1 Arm-chair, 8 little chairs...*

1854　*...for the Center Family—1 little chair...2 Arm chairs ...For the East House—1 candle stand, a Little chair... 1 Dining room bench...*

1856　*...for the Center Family 3 small chairs, 1 arm chair; 4 common chairs & 1 sink. For the East House...3 small chairs, 1 fat press...1 pie safe, 2 tables...For the West Family...4 small chairs,...1 arm chair. For Office 1 small chair & 1 rolling pin.*

1857　*...for the Center Family...1 little chair...For the East House 4 wood boxes...2 Chairs...For the West Family 1 little chair, 1 knife box, 1 Sewing stool.*

In 1859, at the age of seventy six, Brother Francis turned to less demanding tasks. It is noted that he *prepared 25,100 broom handles, 11,400 matches, 711 seed boxes.* His days of chair production were behind him.

During this period the production of chair list or tapes is recorded in the deaconesses' journal *Domestic Concerns.* Entered under the title of *Weaving done* in the year-end summaries at the East House are the following:

1844—Chair list unknown
1846—285 yards of Chair list
1847—575 yards of Chair list
1848—734 yds. of Chair list & carpet binding
1849—344 yds. of Carpet binding and chair list
1850—695 yds. of Chair list & carpet binding
1851—1216 yds. of Chair list & carpet binding
1852—360 yds. of Chair list

A Journal Kept by Polly Harris for the benefit of the Sisters of the West Family records 200 yards of chair list produced in 1844 and 360 yards in 1846.

In *A Temporal Journal...Book B* that reports the production of Monfort is the note that *we have received 4 arm chairs by J. Shain for the use of the Family.* Another *Temporal Journal* entry for May

15, 1854, records, *We received one Doz. boughten Windsor chairs for the family.* An earlier notation in a Pleasant Hill account book mentioned on January 12, 1843, there were *Bought 12 Split Bottom Chairs* for $6.00. Even during the years of greatest recorded production, either necessity or the desire for a style not being made by the Shakers dictated acquiring chairs from the world.

An examination of chairs from Pleasant Hill reveals two variations that differ considerably in overall proportions, shape of pommels, and other features. The first variation is found in the armed rockers, which have bulbous pommels with elongated necks. The deeply bent graduated slats have a boldly shaped contour that flows to a nearly horizontal line before being tenoned into the back posts. The upper two slats are pinned through the back posts and have rounded front edges on the top. The relatively heavy posts are slightly tapered. The symmetrical turning in the front posts between the seat and the arms is tapered at both ends and offers a contrast to the heavier portion below the seat. Three concentric scribe marks appear at the thickest part of this turning. A collar at the top of the front posts meets the side scroll arm behind the scroll. The arms are mortised and pinned into the back posts. The most distinctive feature of these chairs is the handholds that cap the arms. In contrast to eastern chairs, these do not serve as tenon caps to the posts. Screws or wood pegs extend through the center of the handholds into the arms. A screw or peg, approximately halfway between the centered screws or pegs and the outer edges of the handholds, eliminates the possibility of the handholds being twisted or turned. Crescent shaped rockers extend well beyond the front posts.

The second variation of Pleasant Hill chairs occurs in the side chair. In this chair, the back posts culminate in elongated oval pommels, the curved slats are rounded on the front top edges, and only the top slat is secured by wooden pins extending through the posts. The chairs vary in weight as well as in the diameter of the posts. The finest have the seat stretchers pinned at the posts; these are among the most delicate of all Shaker chairs.

T. Monfort has made 2 chairs, 2 Ginnies, 30 tape quills, 1 feather brush & 1 box for the Centre Family; A little table, 2 little chairs, 3 arm chairs, 1 bedstead, 5 feather-brushes, and 30 tape quills for the East Family; 12 spools and 1 Ginny for the West; One little chair for the Office, and 48 spools for the reed shop; besides about 500 sundry small articles and mending &c. for the different Families.

Armed rocker, ca.1830. Side scroll arms without added hand holds. Stocky posts. Hand woven tape. (Shakertown at Pleasant Hill)

Armed rocker, ca. 1840. Top two slats thru pinned. Arms tenoned and pinned into back posts. Front posts tenoned and pinned into arms. Rounded handholds secured with wooden pins at center and midway between center and outer edge. Three scribe marks at swell of turning on front post. Shaped rockers pinned to posts. maple with walnut arms. (Shakertown at Pleasant Hill)

Armed rocker, ca. 1840. Top two slats through pinned. Arms mortised and pinned into backs posts. Front posts mortised into arms. Rounded handholds secured with screw through center and another midway between center and outer edge. Three scribe marks at swell of vase turning on front posts. Black paint over red. (Shakertown at Pleasant Hill)

Extremely delicate side chair, ca. 1850.
Rounded bevel on top edge of slats. Top
slat only through pinned. Seat stretchers
also pinned. Woven seat of blue, red,
white, and light olive. (Shakertown at
Pleasant Hill)

Convenience chair. ca.1830. No turned parts. Slender slats with rounded top front edges. Top slat through pinned. Arms, and small supports beneath them, mortised into back posts. Rounded handholds. Box to hold chamber pot mortised and pinned into posts. (Murphy Collection)

Work chair, ca.1840. Side chair with boots added. Metal collar, probably pewter, on top of boot. Seat height 23⅝. (Shakertown at Pleasant Hill)

(Opposite) Side chair, ca.1840.

SOUTH UNION, KENTUCKY

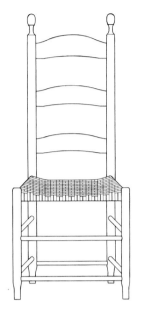

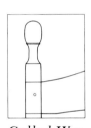

The available resource material relating to chairmaking at South Union suggests production was limited to meeting the needs of the community. Although the journal records state that on April 4, 1822, the *Chair Shop raised,* references to large-scale manufacturing and/or selling from this structure are absent. *Called Wm. Rice's shop,* it stood *East of South from Ministrys shop.*

Since the building bears his name, Rice must have been an early chairmaker at South Union. More than a quarter of a century later, on January 5, 1849, *Journal B, Vol 1* records the names of *Robt. John & R. Wise making them.* Shortly after that date, the 1844-1860 account book lists *Articles bought in Louisville by Eli,* which included *1 Set Turners Gauges 6$—do chisels 4$—10.00* probably used in the production of chairs. A reference on February 8, 1857, to *Robt. Johns making chairs for 2nd order...* is followed shortly by a similar purchase: *Bot in Bowling Green—Set chisels & Gouges for W. Rice 4.45.*

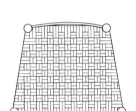

The typical South Union chair is a three-slat side chair with three features that distinguish it from other Shaker chairs: (1) resembling an egg in a cup, the oval-shaped pommels descend to a ridge that creates the cup effect, then reduce in diameter to the typical small neck before broadening to form the shoulders at the top of the posts; (2) the back slats are arched on both top and lower edges, the lower edge has a gentler curve. This concave arch on the lower edge is noticeably chamfered by use of hand tools; (3) beginning at a point approximately one inch below the lowest stretcher, the posts are sharply tapered in a concave curve.

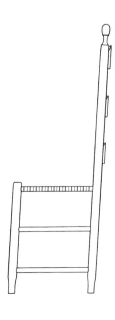

The primary exception to the South Union form is the dining chair. Although heavier in construction, it has two slats and is an obvious variation of the eastern dining chairs. The Church Family journal entry of January 1, 1849, records: *CHAIR for the DINING TABLE—Brethren on this blessed New years day began to make chairs for the dining Room & so get clear of benches.* Chairs were

Side chair, ca.1850. Crisply shaped neck with ridge below large oval pommel. Top back slat through pinned. Boots added to raise seat height. (Shakertown at South Union) Photograph by Clark Rice.

already in use in the dining room of the Second Family, as noted by the July 6, 1839, commentary: *Eli McLean returned home from Nashville bringing chairs for the dining room at the 2nd. Order... having been absent some 5, 6, or 7 days.* The chairs used at South Union were a combination of those made within the community and ones purchased from the world.

Side chair, ca.1840. Top two slats through pinned. Lower edges of slats have a concave curve. Strong concave taper on posts below bottom stretchers. Mustard yellow paint. (Shakertown at South Union) Photograph by Clark Rice.

Child's chair, ca.1840. Boldly shaped slats with concave curve on lower edges. Mustard yellow paint. (Shakertown at South Union) Photograph by Clark Rice.

NEW LEBANON, NEW YORK

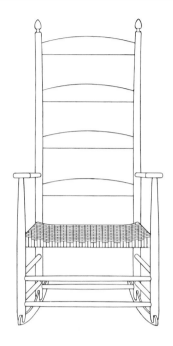

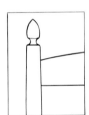

The New Lebanon community was the most prolific in chairmaking in terms of its longevity and volume of production. The November, 1889, *Manifesto* reflects this prominence:

We have spared no expense or labor in our endeavors to produce an article that cannot be surpassed in any respect, and which combines all the advantages of durability, simplicity and lightness. The largest chairs weigh only ten pounds and the smallest less than five.

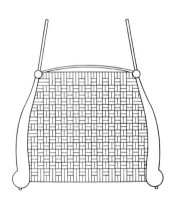

Many of our friends who see the Shakers' chairs for the first time may be led to suppose that the chair business is a new thing for the Shakers to engage in. This is not the fact, however, and may surprise even some of the oldest manufacturers to learn that the Shakers were pioneers in the business, and perhaps the very first to engage in the business after the establishment of the independence of the country.

We have in our possession specimens of chairs made by our people, which, judging from their appearance, would indicate that they were made in revolutionary times, and would adorn any cabinet of antiquities.

The year 1876 is the centennial year of the first Shaker settlement in this country, and the commencement of our chair business is recorded back to this date, as the manufacture of home-made articles were then a necessity, and chair-making has always remained with us an occupation to the present time.

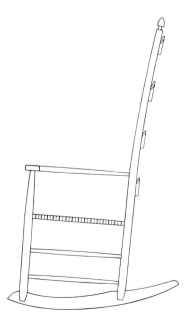

While the catalogue and *Manifesto* references place the manufacturing of chairs in the earliest days of the faith, account book references to chairs are not available until after the formal organization of the Shakers into community order at New Lebanon in 1786. On September 25, 1789, the daybook of Brother Joseph Bennet, Jr., records that *1 Great & 6 Small Chairs* were sold to Brother Elizah Slosson of the Second Family. This sale illustrates the social and economic independence and interrelatedness of the various families. In the first years, many chair sales were made to other segments within the United Society of Believers, but some sales were to persons outside the Shaker community.

Edward D. and Faith Andrews in their books *The Community Industries of the Shakers* and *Shaker Furniture* thoroughly document the available New Lebanon record books showing sales of the early Shaker chairs. In presenting the material pertaining to the last decade of the eighteenth century, they list the following entries from the account book of the Church Family:

> 1790—To Daniel Goodrich (Hancock trustee) 4 chairs at 4/8
>
> 1791 Feby—Delivered to Eliphelet Comstock, in Enfield, Conn.... 6 chairs
>
> Feby 2—To Eleazer Grant (a magistrate in the town of New Lebanon) ... 6 chairs
>
> Novr 10—To Zebulon Goodrich 3 chairs without Bottoms but Painted
>
> 1792 Novr 19—To Timothy Edwards of Stockbridge, Mass. 8 chairs at 3/
>
> 1798—One *"house chair"* delivered to John Shapley

In the early decades of the nineteenth century, chairs were a commodity to be peddled along with oval boxes, brooms, sieves, whips, and spinning wheels. Brothers Nathan and Stephen Slosson of the Church Family made regular trips to many nearby towns, including Albany, Hudson, *Lansbory*, and Petersburg, and traveled as far as Boston to sell their wares. They sold *common rocking chairs, wagan chairs, great chair, high chairs without botoms*, chair frames, small chairs, large rocking chairs, and chair cushions.

The simple design of Shaker chairs was only beginning to develop. It is difficult, and in many cases impossible, to distinguish those early chairs from ones made in the world.

Consistently heavier than chairs of later years, the staid early examples had straight rear posts measuring 1½ to 1⅝ inches in diameter. These terminated in pommels that exhibit little refinement in style or craftsmanship. The pommels are more rounded or bulbous in shape than later variants and are slightly reduced in diameter before dropping to their narrowest point. The back slats are not graduated and are generally flat on the top edge. They often show grain splintering indicating that they had been riven rather than sawn. The stretchers are heavy and straight and do not taper until about 1 inch before being tenoned into the posts.

Work chair, ca.1820. Unusual number of stretchers. Old flag seat. (Private Collection)

Work chair, ca.1820. Extremely wide seat. Two slats are unusual for a work chair. (Courtesy of Hancock Shaker Village, Inc., Pittsfield, Massachusetts)

Side chair, ca.1800-20. Similar to the chair on the previous page without the sausage turnings. Slightly lighter. Leather seat. Red paint. (Courtesy of The Shaker Museum, Old Chatham, New York)

Armed rocker, ca.1800-1820. Possibly New Lebanon or Watervliet, New York. Magnificent mushroom post rocker with fine details and large rockers. (The Nelson Collection)

On armchairs, the front posts taper upwards from the seat to about 1½ to 2 inches below the arms where they abruptly swell to form collars for receiving the arms. The tops of the posts are capped with large mushrooms usually turned as integral parts of the posts. The arms, varying slightly in thickness from front to rear, are crescent-shaped and tenoned into both the front and rear posts. On rocking chairs from these years, the rockers are great in depth, measuring as much as 5 inches at their center points.

Documentation of chair production through account book references during the rest of the first quarter of the century is incomplete, although references confirm the presence of a chairmaking industry in the East Family which, along with the Second Family, had been formed into covenant order on March 26, 1814. The New Lebanon Ministry Sisters Journal records the destruction of the chair shop on August 28 of that same year.

> *This day we had an abundance of rain which raised the streams, and caused great destruction and loss of property. On the stream which supplies the clothiers works, fulling mill and carding machines three dams were carried away ... a considerable quantity of oil in the carding mill, a chair makers shop with a large number of unfinished chairs, stock and tools were all swept away.*

Another journal, that of Brother Freegift Wells who was visiting from Watervliet at the time, refers to the same incident: *John Bishops shop and tools with 20 new waggon chairs were swept off it the deluge it was a melloncholly sight to behold.*

The East and Second Families were branches of the North and Church Families, respectively, at New Lebanon and closely bound historically and geographically. It is difficult to tell whether these families were producing chairs simultaneously or if the industry was shifted between jurisdictions. Journal references pertaining to chairs are very sketchy in the years following the destruction of the East Family's shop and do not appear in any notable numbers until after the construction of the new building, which, according to a news article a century later, took place in 1826. The account books of the Church Family mention numerous purchases from Thomas Estes and, after 1832, William Thrasher, trustees of the East Family.

According to Church Family account books, $6.50 was paid to the Canaan Family for a chair on February 26, 1839. Later that year, November 4, the Canaan Family received $7.50 for *two rocking chairs.*

The construction of chairs by the Canaan Family of New Lebanon can be dated to 1817 as Brother Benjamin Lyon records in his journal on January 3: *Anthony works at a Clockcase. I at chests and dowing chairs.* On January 15, 1836, he writes, *I wor in the shop some a choreing saome a geting out rockers for chares & the weather grores coald.* Three days later, he *Put in rockers in two chares.* It should be noted that all of the entries in Brother Benjamin's journal which related to woodworking were made in the months of November, December or January. The rest of the year, he was involved in planting, hauling manure, harvesting and other activities. For him, as for many other brothers, cabinetry and chairmaking were seasonal occupations.

One of the references to the sale of chairs in the Canaan Family account books states that on July 7, 1845, the community *Rec's of Justic Harwood for 2½ doz. chairs, $28.50.* Brother Justic was a member of the Watervliet community. Another entry lists $13.50 *Rec's of Azariah for chair.* The sales of chairs in this quantity probably indicated greater production than enumerated by the few available records.

By the 1840s, the style of the New Lebanon chair is noticeably lighter, more refined and balanced in its proportions. The rear posts are approximately 1⅜ inches in diameter and taper from the seat up, contributing to the lightness of the chair. The pommels are oval in shape, pointed on the tops, with two well-defined reductions, the lower of which forms the smallest diameter before reaching the shoulders. Little change is evident in the style of the back slats. The front posts on the armchairs have a concave taper above the seat, dropping to about ¾ inch in diameter at the thinnest point. A ridge or well-defined transitional turning precedes a slight taper to the larger, fully formed collar upon which the arm rests. In contrast to the earlier examples where the arms were tenoned into the front and rear posts, the side scroll arms are tenoned only into the rear posts. The fronts of the arms terminate in circular handholds with the posts mortised into the bottom of the handholds. There is little shaping of the edges on these arms.

The much lighter rocker blades, about ⅜ inch thick, have rounded fronts, concave curves on the top between the posts, and then continue in a straight line to a rounded end that begins about ½ inch before meeting the underside. The shape of the rockers on chairs of this period will occasionally vary, as will the base of the front posts. Since the posts have been made lighter than those of the earlier mushroom post chair, the posts often terminate in a boot or swell for receiving the rockers.

Side scroll armchairs of just a few years later exhibit considerable refinement. This is particularly notable in the arms which become much more slender as they approach the rear posts. The outside edges of the arms have developed a fine bevel and the inside edges have been gently rounded.

" . . . Gilbert (Avery) brought in a few hundred dollars by making chairs."
History of the Lower Family, 1843

"Suitable Furniture for Retiring Rooms. And this is the order after which your retiring rooms shall be furnished. Bed steads painted green, Comforters of a brownish shade. Blankets for outside spreads, blue and white, but not checked. Plain-splint, list of tape bottomed chairs are preferable to any other kind. One rocking chair in a room is sufficient except where the aged reside. One or two plain and decent chair mats for every room if desired."

February 18, 1841
from *The Holy Orders of the Church* written by Father Joseph to the elders of church at New Lebanon and copied agreeable to Father Joseph's word.

Armed rocker, ca.1830. Posts lighter than mushroom post, ca.1810, but heavier than later chairs. Side scroll arms slightly rounded on edges and do not have detail of later examples. (Douglas and Cornelia Hamel)

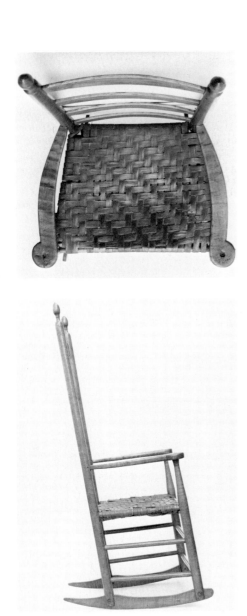

Armed rocker, ca.1830. Possibly New Lebanon or Watervliet, New York. Enlarged turning at the base of the posts provides added strength for the rockers. Wheels added to an already finished rocker. The wheel rims were probably originally fitted with metal or leather on the rim.

(Courtesy of The Shaker Museum, Old Chatham, New York)

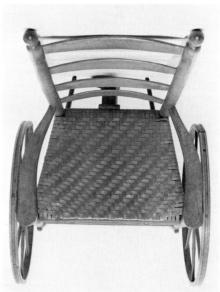

Side chair, ca.1840. Very small child's chair. Only one row of stretchers below the seat because of small size. Height 23¾ inches. (Jerry Grant)

Side chair, ca.1840. Child's chair of more common proportions. Height 28 inches. (Mr. and Mrs. Kenneth F. Brooker)

Side chair, ca.1840. Large child's chair or small adult's. Cane seat. Height 32¼ inches. (Private Collection)

Side chair, ca.1840. Adult chair. Pommel style seen on rocking and side chairs. On these and many other chairs with the same pommel, the top slat is through pinned. On most other New Lebanon chairs the pins are visible only from the back. (Collection of DeGiorgis and VanAlstyne)

Armless rocker, ca.1840. Finely styled short rockers. Old woven tape seat. (Courtesy of The Shaker Museum, Old Chatham, New York)

Side chair, ca.1840. Extremely delicate pommels. Dark green paint. (Art Complex Museum of Duxbury)

Armed rocker, ca.1850. Very early chair to have cushion bar, a feature more common to production chairs after 1860. (Collection of John Keith Russell)

Armed rocker, ca. 1850. Unusually broad seat for a rocking chair of this period. Finely detailed arms. This style of rocker blade was used around 1850-1875. Cane seat. Curly maple. (Courtesy of Hancock Shaker Village Inc., Pittsfield, Massachusetts)

Sisters' bedroom, 1895. A wide variety of chair cushions were used. (Courtesy of The Shaker Museum, Old Chatham, New York)

"How comes it about that there are so many rocking chairs used? Is the rising generation going to be able to keep the way of God, by seeking after ease?"

April 11, 1840
from a message by Philemon Stewart delivered to the ministry and elders at the first order of the Church, New Lebanon

Elder Frederick Evans (1808-1893) of the North Family, ca.1880. Photograph by Irving, Troy, New York. Photograph taken near the large stone barn of the North Family at New Lebanon. Pommels, back and rockers are typical of New Lebanon chairs but the plank bottom chair style is uncommon except for dining chairs. Location of chair unknown. (Courtesy of Hancock Shaker Village, Inc., Pittsfield, Massachusetts)

Deaconesses sewing room, after 1870. Armed rocker with side scroll arms, ca.1840. Armless chair with only the pommels visible. (Courtesy of The Shaker Museum, Old Chatham, New York)

Sisters making bonnets, date unknown. Armed rocker with side scroll arms, ca.1850. (Courtesy of Hancock Shaker Village, Inc., Pittsfield, Massachusetts)

"Shakeresses Labeling and wrapping the Bottles containing the Shaker Extract of Roots." 1885 *Shaker Almanac.* (Courtesy of Hancock Shaker Village, Inc., Pittsfield, Massachusetts)

Packaging herbs, date unknown. (Courtesy of The Shaker Museum, Old Chatham, New York)

SHAKERESSES LABELING AND WRAPPING THE BOTTLES CONTAINING THE SHAKER EXTRACT OF ROOTS, OR SEIGEL'S SYRUP

Lowback dining chairs were used in most Shaker communities. In the second half of the nineteenth century and into the 1900s, many communities purchased chairs manufactured in the outside world for use in the dining rooms. Some of these reflected the style of the Shaker low back chairs while others were chairs readily available in the commercial world.

Low back chairs, ca.1850. Two slats. No pommels. Strongly tapered front posts. Tilters. (The Sherman Collection)

Low back chairs, ca.1830 and 1850. (The Sherman Collection)

Low back chair, ca. 1860. Two slats. Number "2" stamped on back slat helps to date the chair to the years of factory production although this style chair was not made for general sale to the world. (Private Collection)

Low back chair, ca. 1850. Single slat through pinned to posts. Splint seat. (Courtesy of Hancock Shaker Village, Inc., Pittsfield, Massachusetts)

The progress of the chair industry is reflected in the diary entry of Elder James Prescott of North Union upon his visit to New Lebanon on October 5, 1860:

> . . . *the chair making business—they sell a Big Arm Chair with rockers, cushioned, for 12 dollars, and they manufacture a new kind of chair, which turns on a screw pivot, every which way, different kinds and sizes. Then, the Sisters weave the cushions, and pieces to put in, up and down the back of the chairs which gives them a very rich velvet appearance—Grandees, don't value paying 10 or 12 dollars for such a rocking chair, and even take them to England & France. If I could get one of them in my trunk, I would bring home one for Elder Pomeroy and one for Eldress Susannah, but I cannot . . .*

This *new kind of chair* is today called the revolving stool.

On May 20, 1863, the Second Family purchased from the South Family 24 revolving stools for $48. On July 2, another 24 revolving stools were purchased for $60.

These revolving stools were not original with the South Family, as can be seen in the 1863 *Agreement at the time of the division.* A January 18, 1860, entry lists *1 stool chair to Elder S . . .* and *1 stool chair give to Br. Giles,* as well as *1 small turning chair.* The *different kinds and sizes* in Elder James' diary would account for the variance in cost for the stools sold to the Second Family.

The *turning chairs* or *revolving stools* were made in two forms, both having turned and hollowed seats supported by cast metal yokes mounted upon metal swivel shafts. The first variation has a spider base made from two wood arcs that cross in a half-lap joint at the center. Metal screws run through the joint and fasten into the upright or stem which tapers from about 4 inches to 1½ inches at the top. Above the seat is a back composed of six to eight spindles supporting a bent, rounded rail. The spindles on later models are often metal rods. Occasionally, the revolving stools have no backs. The seat height is usually adjustable.

The second variation is Windsor in form, having four legs joined together with two sets of stretchers mortised into swollen turnings. Two cross-members receive the legs near their ends and are joined with a half-lap joint at the point of support for the swivel shaft. The back is like that of the spider base variation. These chairs are often not adjustable for elevation.

Revolving stool, ca.1860. Refined spider base. Finely bent and tapered spindles set into bent rail. Concave/convex taper on pedestal with metal collar on top. Adjustable seat height. Mixed woods. (Private Collection)

1 Revolving stool, ca.1880. Spindles tapered but almost straight. Spider base not as heavy or arched as earlier examples. Adjustable seat height. (The Sherman Collection)

2 Revolving stool, ca.1920. Not as finely made as earlier revolvers. Base is crudely shaped and pedestal has a simple straight taper. Seat is only slightly hollowed, then rounded on outside edge. Metal spindles. Seat height adjustable. (From the Collection of the United Society of Shakers, Sabbathday Lake, Maine)

3 Revolving stool, date unknown. Very unusual base of forged metal with penny feet. Legs inserted into wood pedestal.

Back spindles and rail removed. Mixed woods. Adjustable seat height. (Courtesy of Hancock Shaker Village, Inc., Pittsfield, Massachusetts)

4 Revolving stool, ca.1920. Plush cushion material same as used on cushions for production chairs. (The Sherman Collection)

1

2

3

4

1 Revolving stool, ca.1860. Very short rail with only six spindles. Seat height not adjustable. (Courtesy of Hancock Shaker Village, Inc., Pittsfield, Massachusetts)

2 Revolving stool, ca.1860. Child's high chair with deeply bent round rail fitted to tapered and bent spindles. Curved foot rest. Grace- ful leg turnings. Exquisite stool. Seat height adjustable. (Courtesy of The Henry Ford Museum, Dearborn, Michigan)

3 Revolving stool, 1875-1900. Deeply bent shaped rail fitted to angled spindles with enlarged turnings at base. Seat mounted to shaft by wood cleat rather than metal flange. Extra turnings on heavily splayed legs. Height not adjustable. (Courtesy of New York State Museum, Albany, New York)

4 Revolving stool, ca.1860. Very tall elongated base. Seat height not adjustable. Seat height 38 inches. (Courtesy of Hancock Shaker Village, Inc., Pittsfield, Massachusetts)

1

2

3

4

Revolving armed rocker, ca.1860. An incredible combination of a side scroll armed rocker and a revolving stool base on rockers. The chair is now in the collection of The Western Reserve Historical Society, Cleveland, Ohio. (Index of American Design [OHIO - FU-24]; National Gallery of Art, Washington, D.C.)

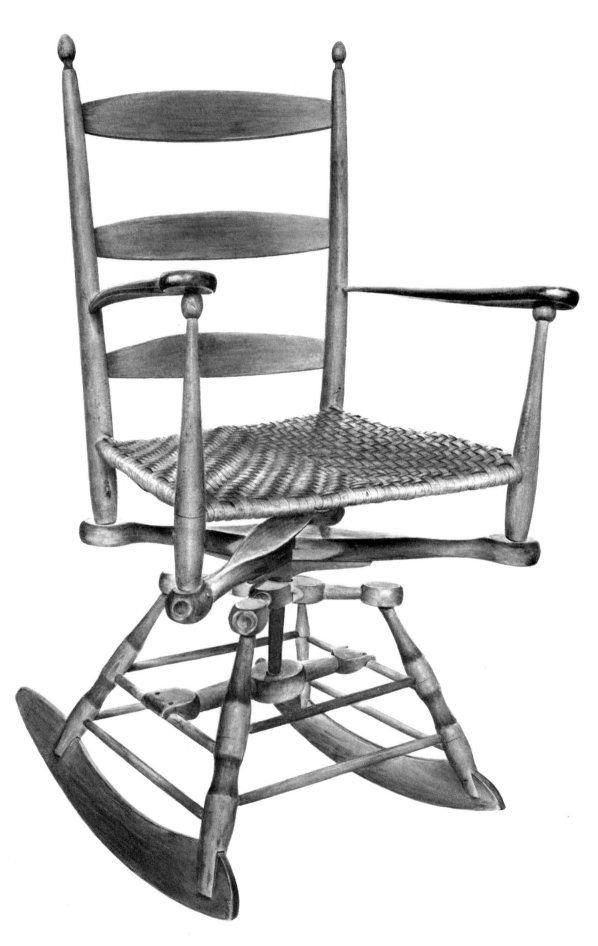

Convenience chair, ca.1860. Variation of the revolver style. Tin chamber pot is removable by adjusting a lever beneath it. Very fine construction. Signed "Jas. Smith." (The Stokes Collection)

While the first half of the nineteenth century provides only limited information on chair production at the Church, East, Canaan, and Second families, the second half is more extensively documented. Various records of the chair industry that developed in the Second Family and, later, at the South Family give information regarding the shift in location and volume of manufacture. The inventories of stock held at the beginning of 1852 mention the East Family with *chair cushion — $46*. Ten years later, the inventory of the Second Family showed *160 chairs for market*. During this decade, that family sold its chairs to the Church Family and to the neighboring community of Hancock: January 6, 1853—*6 chairs for $9;* April 12, 1853—*14 chairs for $14;* 1857—*2 common sitting chairs for $2* and *2 sewing chairs for frames for $2.50.*

The midpoint in the century marked the rise to prominence of the Second Family as the leader in the chair business. The growth in the production of chairs by this family can be seen in inventory records and a change in marketing methods — the use of a broadside.

The earliest known chair broadside or price list is dated 185- and indicates a standardization permitting early mass production and marketing methods. Both splint and tape seats are advertised along with the option of cushions at an extra cost. An additional option — one that does not appear in later known catalogues — was *button joint tilts,* now commonly called tilters.

Tilters can be found on many early chairs although the date when they were first used by the Shakers is difficult to determine. Brother Freegift writes in his journal on September 27, 1819, that he begins *to trim off and ball the chairs,* which might be interpreted as buttons. Brother Benjamin Lyon refers in his journal to January 20, 1836, as *a day to doe chores doe some in the shop at making buttens to put in the bottum of chares poasts or (nubs) to keep from maring the floor.*

Some chairs existing today with the ball-and-socket mechanism in the rear legs date from the beginning of the eighteenth century. The presence of buttons on early examples, the widespread use of the mechanism throughout other communities, and the reference in an 185- price list indicates that buttons were common to Shaker chairs during the second quarter of the nineteenth century. This date seems proper since patent No. 8771 for a refined version of the *chair feet* was issued on March 2, 1852, to George O. Donnell, a New Lebanon brother. The patent application reflects the wording in the journal entry of Brother Benjamin sixteen years earlier, when it states that the invention is *a new and improved mode of preventing the wear and tear of carpets and the marring of floors, caused by the corners of the back posts of chairs.*

On a very few chairs, the button tilt joints were made according to the exact description in the patent specifications, where the foot is a separate piece riveted onto the shank of the ball. On most chairs, the button tilt ball is a solid piece combining the ball and foot. On a small number of chairs, the ball, as well as the ferrule which holds the button in the hollowed end of the post, is made of pewter and/or brass. Most of these are side chairs of tall proportions and of figured

We drove up to one of the houses, and were received at the door by a respectable elderly female dressed in a brown coloured dress. Mr. Clinton had given Mr. Owen a letter of introduction to the Society, which he delivered and was led into a small neat room, with small woolen carpets on the floor, the walls white, the wood work stained a brownish red colour & the chairs of stained wood, the seats of them of strips of ash wood, and the window blinds of a blue stuff. . . . We sat and conversed some minutes with this sister who had a chair with the feet so made as to rock back & forward.

The Diaries of Donald MacDonald, 1824-1826

PRICE LIST
OF
SHAKERS CHAIRS.

Manufactored in the UNITED SOCIETY,

NEW LEBANON, Columbia Co. N. Y.

For the Year 185

		$	cts.
LARGE size armed rocking chair. . *Frame*		3	25
MEDIUM size, ...		3	00
SMALL do, ...		2	75
DINING do, ...		2	00
EASY do, ...		2	00
COMMON or **Kitchen,**		1	00
CHILDREN'S, ...			75

		cts.
☞ SPLINT Seat for Arm Chair,		50
do do do Common,		38
do do do Children's,		25
TAPE seat for the above named varieties of CHAIRS, . . .		1 00
For Rockers, ...		50
do Button joint TILTS, . .		25
CUSHIONS Extra, at fair prices.		

JESSE LEWIS.
D.C. BRAINARD.

Patent drawing. Mar. 2, 1852.

woods. Sometimes a brass ferrule will bear the patent date. One side
scroll armchair has the metal ferrule stamped *Pat. 1852.*

The most common variation of the *button joint tilts* uses a
button turned from wood, with no ferrule. This is seen on the earlier
chairs as well as those from the later years of mass production.
Without the metal ferrule to hold the button in place, a leather thong
was used to secure the button in the socket. It was knotted and drawn
through a hole in the button, threaded through a drilled hole in the
side post, then fastened with a tack or small tapered wood peg. On
New Lebanon chairs, the hole usually consisted of two channels: one
drilled straight up through the center of the post; the second
extending from the center at a 20 to 30-degree angle to the exterior
where it exited about 1 or 2 inches from the bottom of the post.

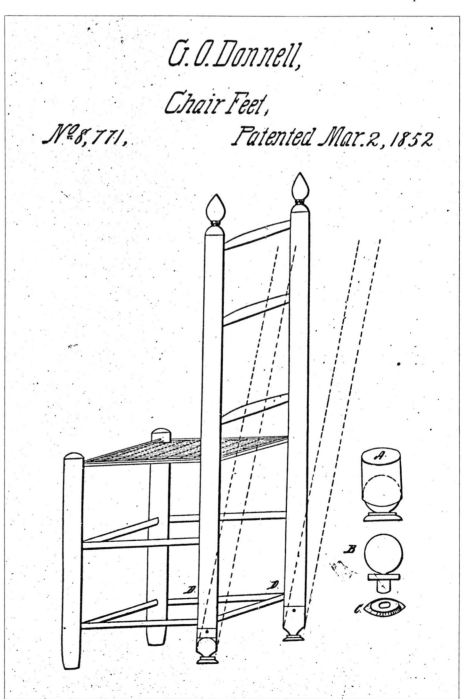

Model chair and paper label for the button joint tilt. Dated Mar. 2, 1852. (Antiquities of Lexington)

United States Patent Office Specifications. March 2, 1852.

UNITED STATES PATENT OFFICE.

GEO. O. DONNELL, OF NEW LEBANON, NEW YORK.

CHAIR.

Specification of Letters Patent No. 8,771, dated March 2, 1852.

To all whom it may concern:

Be it known that I, GEORGE O. DONNELL, of Shaker village, in the town of New Lebanon, in the county of Columbia and State 5 of New York, have invented a new and improved mode of preventing the wear and tear of carpets and the marring of floors, caused by the corners of the back posts of chairs as they take their natural motion of 10 rocking backward and forward; and I do hereby declare that the following is a full and exact description thereof, reference being had to the accompanying drawing and to the letters of reference marked thereon.

15 The nature of my invention consists in a metallic ferrule, ball, and foot piece, combined; and applied to the back posts of a chair in such a manner, as to let the chair take its natural motion of rocking backward 20 and forward, while the metallic foot piece rests unmoved; flat and square on the floor or carpet.

To enable others skilled in the art to make and use my invention, I will proceed to de-25 scribe its construction and operation.

I firstly cut my ferrule with a die; it is then bent to a mandrel and brazed; then it is swaged in a socket so as to contract the lower end (as shown at A, in the accompanying drawing) sufficiently to hold the 30 ball B, which is dropped partially through the ferrule A, so as to receive the foot piece C, which is riveted onto the shank of the ball B. Thus is the metallic combination completed and ready to apply to the back 35 posts of a chair as shown on the chair posts D. The ball B is cast and finished in the lathe, and the foot piece C is cut with a die like unto the ferrule A.

What I claim as my invention and desire 40 to secure by Letters Patent, is—

The construction, and application of a metallic combination, to the back posts of chairs; so as to let the chairs take their natural motion, of rocking backward and 45 forward, while the metallic feet rest unmoved; flat and square on the floor or carpet; or any other metallic affixion substantially the same, and which will produce the intended motion.

GEORGE O. DONNELL.

Witnesses:
JEREMIAH TALLCOTT,
D. J. HAWKINS.

Side chairs, ca.1850. Rare pair of chairs
with metal tilters like those on the patent
model. Extreme backward tilt defined by
the angle that the side stretchers are mortised
into the posts. (The Sherman Collection)

Side chair, ca.1850. Pewter tilting ball. Brass ferrules marked "Patent 1852." Ball secured with leather thong. (Courtesy of New York State Museum, Albany, New York)

Armed chair, ca.1852. Brass tilter ferrule marked "Patent 1852." Chair is similar to a No. 5 armchair advertised in the chair catalogs of the 1870s. (Private Collection)

Side chairs, ca.1850. Pair with metal ferrules. Slight concave curve on bottom of back slats is unusual. Birdseye maple. A similar chair is dated 1848. (The Sherman Collection)

Side chair, ca. 1850. Exquisite proportions combined with pewter ferrules and tilter balls to make this a superb chair. Cane seat. Figured maple and birch. (Courtesy of The Shaker Museum, Old Chatham, New York)

Side chair, 1853. Date stamped on front post is helpful in dating other chairs by comparing back slats, pommels, and taper on front posts. (Courtesy of Hancock Shaker Village, Inc., Pittsfield, Massachusetts)

Shaker Village, Mt. Lebanon, N. Y. looking North.

With the new factory properly functioning, Wagan is reported on March 30, 1875, as *having the old chair factory torn down.*

As noted in *The Shaker,* the new factory building included housing for some of the employees. An account book reference for February 6, 1873, indicates payment for insurance on the factory tenement. The same account book includes contracts for several hired hands who worked in the chair factory.

March 24, 1871—Hugh Gallagher agrees to work 1 year from April 1st for $20 per mo. his food and lodging and 50 cts. per mo. toward his washing.

May 1874—Frank Shaw begins work at varnishing chairs for $25 per month and his food and lodging.

April 1875—Alexander Beckworth commences to work for $18 per month, his food and lodging the year round if we have work in the chair factory.

April 8, 1884—Alexander Smith for labor one year less lost time in full $356.00

June 5, 1884—Orra Wright, Labor at chair factory $39.00.

March 23, 1889—Samuel Wilde, Labor at varnishing chairs, $4.90.

November 29, 1890—Wm. E. Merry, varnishing & painting chairs $4.90

December 16, 1890—John Dermody, Seating chairs by wife $14.22

Checks written on the Agricultural National Bank of Pittsfield by R.M. Wagan & Co. show payments to employees well into the twentieth century. Checks for *labor* were made out to Harry Cornelius, Michael Shea, Nelson Foote, Timothy Buckley, Aaron Sedgwick, Wm. Allen, Ernest Potter, Charles Potter, Archibald McCullock, Lewis Hendricks, Henry Dudley, M. Gaylord, W. Dearborn and, in April of 1910, George W. Lasty, H.E. Finkle, and A.L. Tinker.

The development of mass production methods and the increase in output brought standardization and uniformity. The earliest account books designate chair variations as *small chair frames, large rocker,* and *common chair.* These terms continue to be used in the 185- price list and the pre-1874 list which describes the chairs by size and/or function; for example, *sewing chair, easy chair, large rocker.* Some account books in the early 1860s begin to show the change in terminology toward the numerical system where sizes were designated by number with *0* being the smallest and *7* the largest.

An 1860 invoice from New Lebanon shows this change:

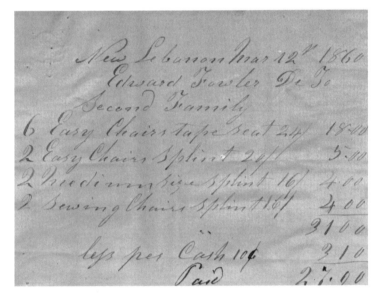

No of Chairs and the prices of the same left at the 2nd Family to be disposed of as per agreement at the time of the division March 24th 1863

No 7	Arm Chairs with rockers	28/- 47	#7	164 50
" 6	" " " "	24	24/-	72 00
" 6	Easy " Broad seat "	145	16/-	290 00
" "	" " " " no rockers	9	12/-	13 50
" "	" " " " High back	24	20/-	60 00
" 5	Dining " no Rockers with arms	31	16/-	62 00
" 3	Chair with Rocker	2	12/-	3 00
" 3	" no "	38	8/-	38 00
" 2	" " "	29	12/-	43 50
" "	" no "	2	8/-	2 00
" 4	Arm Rocking chairs	26	20/-	72 50
" 1	Chairs with Rockers	23	8/-	23 00
	Piano Stools	6	16/-	6 00
	Childrens Revolvers	26	12/-	39 00
	Total	432		889 00
	Less for Varnishing			216 00
			$	673 00

Executive Mansion,

Washington, August 8th 1864.

My good friends:

I wish to express to you my cordial thanks for the very comfortable chair you sent me some time since, and to tell you how gratefully I appreciate the kindness which prompted the present.

And I must beg that you will pardon the length of time that, through an oversight in my office, has elapsed without an acknowledgment of your kindness.

I am very truly
Your friend & obt servt.
A. Lincoln

The agreement at the time of the division of the South Family from the Second Family also illustrates the early use of the numerical classifications, often in combination with designations by function. Within the next decade, the numerical notations became prominent and the use of terminology such as *sewing* and *easy* began to wane. A catalogue dated 1874 with numerical designations continues to retain the earlier descriptions. For example, a No. 3 is listed with the comment that *This is a favorite sewing chair.* The No. 4 is followed by the recommendation that *This is a great favorite with the ladies. It is broad on the seat and very easy.* Later catalogues delete all references to these early functions. The post-1875 catalogue clearly shows the complete acceptance of the new numerical notation.

The chair catalogues were expansions upon the broadsides. The earliest known catalogue is dated 1874, although an illustrated price sheet predates the catalogue by five to ten years. Numerous styles of catalogues were printed in 1875 and 1876 by several commercial printers. In January, 1875, W.P. & Co. (Weed, Parsons & Company of Albany, New York) received $32.43 for woodcuts and stereotypes, and another $67.85 for printing. On October 7, 1876, the sum of $220.50 was paid for catalogues. Thirteen days later, another $169 was listed as paid to *Catalogs WP & CO.* Other catalogues were printed by B.F. Reynolds, Book, Card and Job Printer of Lebanon Springs, New York (1875), and George Denny of Pittsfield, Massachusetts (post-1876).

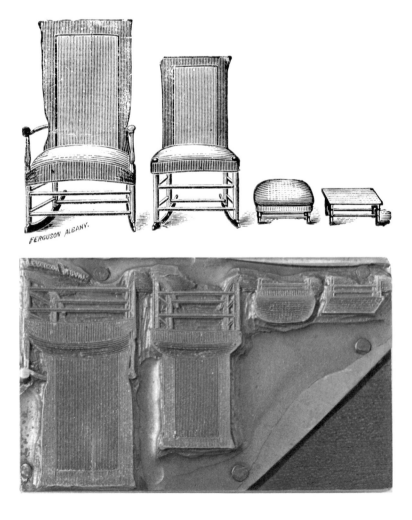

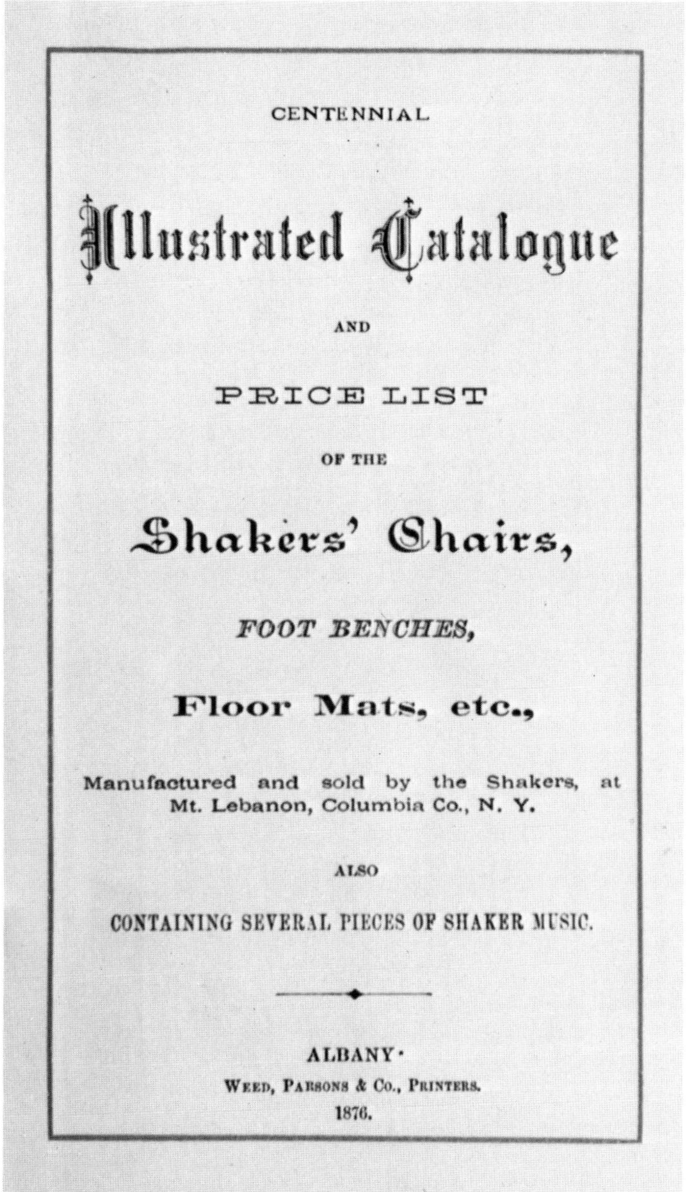

CENTENNIAL

Illustrated Catalogue

AND

PRICE LIST

OF THE

Shakers' Chairs,

FOOT BENCHES,

Floor Mats, etc.,

Manufactured and sold by the Shakers, at Mt. Lebanon, Columbia Co., N. Y.

ALSO

CONTAINING SEVERAL PIECES OF SHAKER MUSIC.

ALBANY·
WEED, PARSONS & CO., PRINTERS.
1876.

The catalogue prepared for the Philadelphia Centennial Exhibition in 1876 is larger in dimensions (4¼″ x 7″) and in total pages (43) than most other examples (2¾″ x 4½″ and 14 to 18 pages). Special engravings in this catalogue show the exhibition buildings, Shaker songs, and advertising by retail firms selling Shaker chairs and other products. A South Family journal reads on April 7, *the Centennial things* (were taken) *to the depot.* Three days later, *Robert & Ora Wright went to Philadelphia to set up the Centennial things. Staid 4 days.* Later in the month, April 29, *Robert Wa. went to Philadelphia to set his chairs right.* The chairs were awarded a *Diploma & Medal at the Centennial Exhibition,* a fact cited in later chair catalogues.

Numerous requests for catalogues show up in the chair order books. An order from the Thayer & Toby Company in Chicago, dated November 3, 1874, requests *3 Sett cushions No 1,* and then adds, *Send at once with Cuts & Price Lists.* Another entry, Newman and Co. of New York City, has the notation, *Send Catalogues. Soon as possible.* Marshall Field and Co. of Chicago used at least two catalogues printed under its name. Both used engravings from the standard chair catalogue of New Lebanon.

Another firm, Gudeons of Philadelphia, listed chairs in their advertisement for Shaker woodenware items which appeared in Atkinson's *Saturday Evening Post.*

The Shakers did some advertising in commercial periodicals, as is shown by a small display advertisement in the May 29, 1875, issue of *Harper's Weekly.* An entry in an account book notes that $13.34 was paid on December 20, 1877, for *Advertising Harpers.*

SHAKERS' WEB-SEATED CHAIRS.

Manufactured and sold by the Society at Mount Lebanon, N. Y. Every chair of our make bears a gold transfer trademark, and none others are genuine. Send for our Illustrated Catalogue and Price-List. Address R. M. WAGAN, Mount Lebanon, N. Y.

Page from 1876 chair catalogue showing exhibition hall in Philadelphia World's Fair. (Courtesy of The Shaker Museum, Old Chatham, New York)

Diploma awarded to the Shakers for their chairs at the 1876 World's Fair. (Courtesy of New York State Museum, Albany, New York)

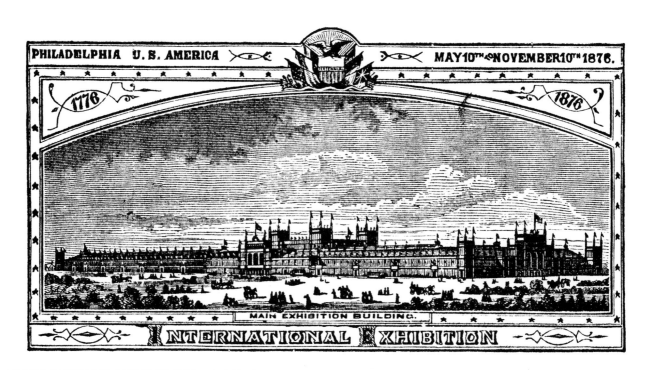

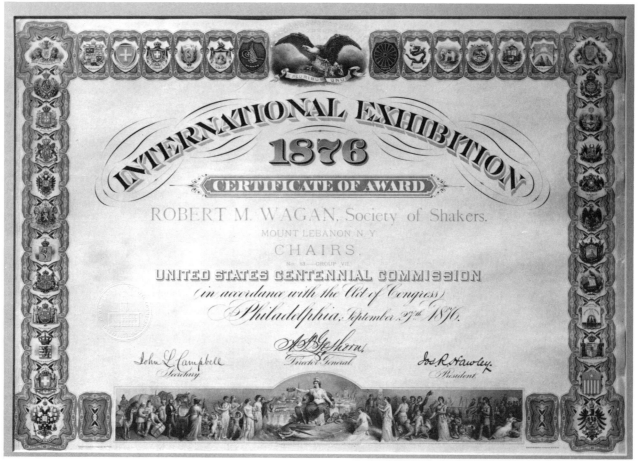

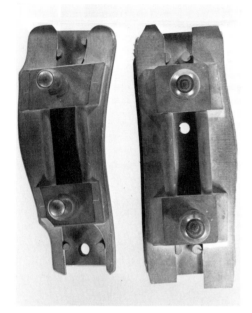

The chair catalogues changed with the development of the industry and, therefore, are useful in analyzing the transition of style in the chairs of the production period. Although not showing the chairs with absolute accuracy, the engravings used to illustrate the chairs show a progression of changes in construction and design details. Several engravings, particularly those by the commercial engraver Hiram Ferguson in nearby Albany, were used in catalogues beyond the years when the particular style was actually being made.

The changes in chair design and construction documented in the catalogue illustrations were the result of the increased use of specialized machinery. Through the use of jigs and boring machines, the locating of holes for back slats and rungs was mechanically guided, thus eliminating the scribe marks made by the craftsman while the posts were still on the lathe. Jigs were also used for holding the arms as they were given form by a shaper driven by water or steam power.

The replacement of hand-craftsmanship by machine work is apparent on the back slats where the top and bottom edges were rounded over the full length of the slats. Those on earlier chairs were squared-off on the ends and fitted into correspondingly squared slots in the back posts. The rounded slats of the later production chairs were fitted into slots with rounded top and bottom edges that had been cut with a boring machine. Turnings were simplified to accommodate the use of early production duplicating lathes. Extra ring turnings were eliminated from the pommels as well as from the vase turnings on the front posts beneath the arms. Mushroom-shaped tenon-cap handholds, now applied, were simplified and standardized.

The 1874, 1875, and 1876 catalogues show two basic chairs: first, chairs made by the use of many production methods, but still having style characteristics from earlier years and construction features requiring a considerable amount of handwork; second, chairs where tooling was done completely by machine, but not yet completely standardized. Later catalogues show a third basic chair which can be considered the R.M. Wagan "standard" production piece. The chair illustrations show in several stages the transition of the chairmaking enterprise from the small "handmade" shop to a mass production factory.

The No. 6 chair illustrated in the 1874 catalogue reflects the first or transitional style maintaining features of the handcrafted chairs while introducing mass production techniques. Stark but buoyant, these chairs represent the finest of man in meeting his seating needs with the greatest economy of materials. The top edge of the slats and the general design of the front posts, arms, and rockers are indicative of the earlier preproduction style. The top edges of the back slats are slightly beveled. The side scroll arms are rounded on the inside and beveled on the outside. The arms taper in thickness from front to back, a hand-finishing detail not duplicated on the later production chairs. It is in the back posts where the first evidence of production era design is seen. They possess simply and uniformly turned pommels, lack scribe marks, and are bent. The bent back post simplifies drilling by creating a 90-degree angle between the side stretchers and the posts.

ca.1874

By contrast, the chairs illustrated by the Ferguson engravings in the 1875 catalogue show the second style—chairs produced totally by factory methods. These chairs are quite slender in all proportions. The front and rear posts are turned to smaller diameters (1¼ inches) than those of later production chairs. The rear posts have a continuous and graceful bend topped by nicely rounded acorn-shaped pommels which vary throughout this period. The back slats are rounded on the top and bottom, as is the case on all later production chairs. The thin arms, reminiscent of the very early crescent style, are formed in a graceful arc. The front posts are tenoned through the arms and capped with oversized mushroom-shaped tenon caps which are wider than the arms themselves. All stretchers are tapered. The rockers are thin blades, fastened to the posts with wood pins, and have curved tops extending from the rear posts, which duplicate the curvature found between the posts.

ca.1875

The third basic style, the R.M. Wagan "standard," is best seen in the post-1876 catalogues in which several new larger engravings were used. The chair of Brother Robert Wagan's reorganized industry was of heavier and bolder proportions than its predecessors and rigid in presence. The rear posts bend prominently just above the seat, but continue with a lesser degree of curve up to the top of the posts. The pommels are a standard acorn-shaped form, which was easily executed by grooving a collar in the post and turning the top of the post to a point. The arm style is broad and flat of uniform thickness with projections at the wrist and elbow positions. The inside and outside edges are identically rounded by a single shaper cutter. The mushroom-shaped tenon caps or handholds are simplified and all stretchers are tapered. The rocker form is standardized with blades terminating in curves on the front and back, and fastened to the posts with flathead screws, a strong and efficient method.

In the 1880's, chair rounds were purchased from outside firms and the taper in the side and rear stretchers gave way to straight dowels which changed in diameter only at the tenons as they entered the posts.

post 1876

Catalogue print and transitional chairs; 1870-80. During the transition from the handmade to the production chair, a variety of designs was tried. These transitional chairs have square edges on the back slats, bent back posts, side scroll arms, and simple tapered front posts. Two styles of rocker blades were produced and are illustrated here.

1 **Engraving of No. 5 armchair.** (Courtesy of The Shaker Museum, Old Chatham, New York)
2 **Chair catalogue, 1876.** (Courtesy of The Shaker Museum, Old Chatham, New York)
3 **Armed rocker. No. 5.** Early transitional rocker with a rocker style used primarily after 1880. (Courtesy of Hancock Shaker Village, Inc. Pittsfield, Massachusetts)
4 **Armless rocker. No. 3.** (Courtesy of Hancock Shaker Village, Inc., Pittsfield, Massachusetts.)
5 **Armchair with tilters, No. 6.** (The Collection of Robert and Katharine Booth. Photograph by Karl Ott)

1

No. 6.

This is the next size smaller than the No. 7, and will answer the same purpose for all who desire a less size. The only difference is in the width and depth of the seat.

We have this chair with or without rockers or arms. See price list.

2

3

4

5

Catalogue print and transitional chairs, 1870-80. A second type of transitional chairs has rounded edges on the back slats, bent back posts, thin crescent shaped arms with mushroom shaped tenon caps and front posts tapered to a slender size where they are mortised into the arms.

1 Chair catalogue, 1876. (Courtesy of The Shaker Museum, Old Chatham, New York)

2 Armed rocker. No. 3. (From the Collection of the United Society of Shakers, Sabbathday Lake, Maine)

3 Armed rocker. No. 6. (Courtesy of the New York State Museum, Albany, New York)

No. 7.

This is our largest chair, and on the top of the back posts is a bar which we attach to all the chairs which are designed for cushions.

We have this chair with or without rockers or arms. See price list.

1

3

2

Catalogue print and transitional chairs, 1875-80. A third type of transitional chair has the vase turning on the front posts of arm chairs. This is the earliest that this turning is used on production Shaker chairs. These chairs have acorn shaped pommels, back slats with rounded top edges, crescent shaped arms, and several styles of mushroom shaped tenon caps.

1 **Armed rocker. No. 3.** (Art Complex Museum of Duxbury)

2 **Chair catalogue, ca.1880.** (Timothy D. Rieman)

3 **Armed rocker. No. 3.** Fine detail in the vase turning and the tenon cap. (Art Complex Museum of Duxbury)

4 **Armchair. No. 6.** Detail showing shape of arm. (Collection of DeGiorgis and Van-Alystene)

5 **Armchair. No. 6.** (Collection of DeGiorgis and VanAlystene)

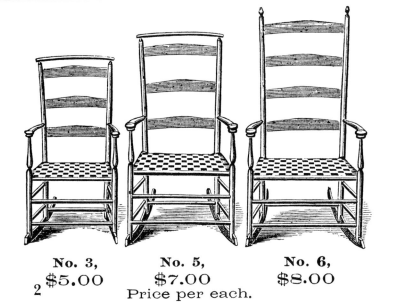

No. 3, $5.00   No. 5, $7.00   No. 6, $8.00
Price per each.

1 Catalogue prints and production chairs, 1880-1920. This chair form was used for decades with only slight variations. The earliest of these had lighter posts than the later examples, tapered stretchers, and, for a few years, crescent shaped arms. The standard Robert Wagan production chair had crisp acorn shaped pommels, bent back posts, rounded edges on the back slats, arms with projections at the wrist and elbow, mushroom shaped tenon caps, a standardized vase turning on the front posts, and one style of rocker blade.

2 Side chair. No. 3. (Art Complex Museum of Duxbury)

3 Armed rocker. No. 5. (Collection of DeGiorgis and Van Alstyne)
4 Armed rocker. No 6. (Collection of DeGiorgis and Van Alstyne)
5 Armed rocker. No. 6. (Courtesy of Charles Flint)
6 Armed rocker. No. 3. (Art Complex Museum of Duxbury)

With the success of the Shaker chair industry, imitations were soon on the market. The 1874 catalogue contained the following warning:

> *Beware of imitation chairs which are sold for our make, and which are called Shakers' chairs. Read, and remember where you can send for the Shakers' chairs and get the genuine. Send your orders to headquarters, as we have only one price and quality to all consumers, and by this shall all men know that they are getting the genuine article*

The 1875 catalogue included a similar warning and added a paragraph of displeasure for those furniture dealers who handled the imitation along with the Shaker chairs.

We would also call the attention of the public to the fact that there is no other chair manufactory which is owned and operated by the Shakers except the one which is now in operation and owned and operated the Society of Shakers at Mount Lebanon, Columbia Co. N.Y. We deem it a duty we owe to the public to enlighten them in this matter, owing to the fact that there are now several manufacturers of chairs who have made and introduced in the market an imitation of our own styles of chairs, which they sell for Shakers' chairs, and which are unquestionably bought by the public generally under the impression that they are the real genuine article made by the Shakers at their establishment in Mount Lebanon, N.Y. Of all the imitations of our chairs which have come under our observation, there is none which we would be willing to accept as a specimen of our workmanship, nor would we be willing to stake our reputation on their merits.

There are a few House Furnishing and Furniture Dealers in some of the principal cities of the country to whom we sell our chairs, and some of those we have recently ascertained do keep and sell the imitation chairs, very much to our disgust and disapprobation; and all such we intend hereafter to discard and withdraw from them our trade, so that the public may be more secure in the purchase of the genuine article when purchasing of the dealers.

Sometime between the printing of the 1874 and 1875 catalogues, the Shakers introduced a trademark for the chair industry that would help customers distinguish their products from the imitators. Although the trademark itself does not appear in the catalogues until after 1876, the statement is made in the 1875 catalogue, and thereafter, that *All Chairs of our make will have a Gold Transfer Trade Mark attached to them and none others are Shakers' Chairs.* An admonition also appeared with the suggestion: *Look for our trademark before purchasing—no chair is genuine without it.*

These transfers will be found on the inside of a rocker or rear post or, most often, on a back slat. They were occasionally applied to the front of the slats where they might be covered with the optional cushion.

On November 26, 1877, the sum of $11.40 was paid *For Trade Marks.* An additional $30 was spent on December 31 of that same year for the same purpose. Palm, Fechteler & Company of New York City was a source for these. Thirty dollars was paid to this firm for *Trade Mark, transfers* on August 14, 1885, and more than twenty years later, transfers were still being purchased from the same company. A cancelled check for March 4, 1908, shows $99.10 for an order of 10,000.

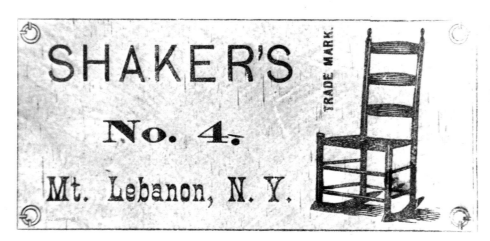

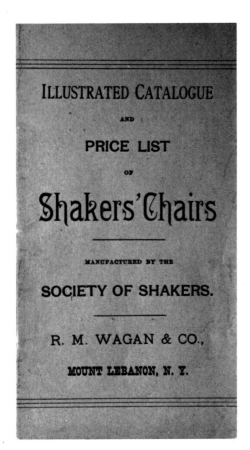

ILLUSTRATED CATALOGUE

AND

PRICE LIST

OF

Shakers' Chairs

MANUFACTURED BY THE

SOCIETY OF SHAKERS.

R. M. WAGAN & CO.,

MOUNT LEBANON, N. Y.

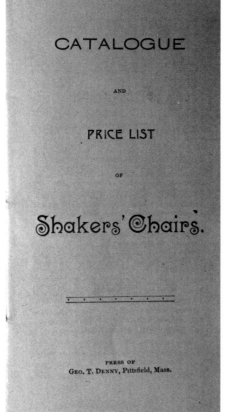

CATALOGUE

AND

PRICE LIST

OF

Shakers' Chairs.

PRESS OF
GEO. T. DENNY, Pittsfield, Mass.

DIRECTIONS

FOR

ORDERING CHAIRS.

As frequent delays and disappointments ensue from a neglect to send definite orders, we are lead to request that you will state the number of chairs wanted, as per illustration.

State definitely the Arms and Rockers. Do you wish both, either, or neither. We do not make the number four with arms; but all other numbers with or without arms and rockers, or with neither arms nor rockers.

State the color of material to be used in seat and back, using number or letter.

The bars across the top of back posts are intended for cushions, but will be furnished to order without additional cost.

State the color of frame wished, as Mahogany, Ebony, or White finish—that is the natural color of the maple wood, for either style the price is the same.

Please send, when you can, shipping orders as to route, railroad, boat, etc., or as freight or express. Attention to these points will oblige.

INTRODUCTION.

WE INVITE the attention of our customers and the public to the contents of this little pamphlet which will give them, in a "concise form," a description and a representation of the different sizes of chairs and foot benches which we manufacture and sell. We would also call the attention of the public to the fact that there is no other chair manufactory which is owned and operated by the Shakers, except the one which is now in operation and owned and operated by the Society of Shakers at Mount Lebanon, Columbia County, N. Y. We deem it a duty we owe the public to enlighten them in this matter, owing to the fact that there are now several manufacturers of chairs who have made and introduced into market an imitation of our styles of chairs, which they sell for Shakers' Chairs, and which are unquestionably bought by the public generally under the impression that they are the real genuine article, made by the Shakers at their establishment in Mount Lebanon, N. Y. Of all the imitations of our chairs which have come under our observation, there are none which we would be willing to accept as our workmanship, nor would we be willing to stake our reputation on their merits.

The increasing demand for our chairs has prompted

4.   INTRODUCTION.

us to increase, also, the facilities for producing and improving them. We have spared no expense or labor in our endeavors to produce an article that cannot be surpassed in any respect, and which combines all the advantages of durability, simplicity and lightness.

Since the establishment of our new factory we have been using a very expensive and durable material in the seating of our chairs, with a great variety of colors.

Many of our friends who see the Shakers' chairs for the first time may be led to suppose that the chair business is a new thing for the Shakers to engage in. This is not the fact, however, and may surprise even some of the oldest manufacturers to learn that the Shakers were pioneers in the business after the establishment of the independence of the country.

The heavy wool plush with which we cushion our chairs is a material peculiarly our own. It is made of the best stock and woven in hand looms, and forms a heavy and durable article much more so than anything we are acquainted with. We have all the most desirable and pretty colors represented in our cushions, and they can be all one color, or have a different color border, or with different colored stripes running across the cushion.

We cushion the foot benches to match the cushioned chairs. They are twelve inches square on top with an incline to favor one's feet while sitting in the chair, and they are nicely adapted for the purpose of kneeling stools.

INTRODUCTION.   5

When any of our friends wish any of our chairs they can order them of us by mail, addressed to R. M. WAGAN & Co., Mt. Lebanon, N. Y. Our chairs are all nicely wrapped in paper before shipping. It is advisable to ship the chairs by express when there are only a few of them. The expense will be more, but the risk will be less than by freight. We do not ship any goods at our own risk, but deliver them at the nearest or most accessible place of shipping, and there take a receipt for them, showing that they were received in good order, when our obligation ends.

Look for our trade-mark before purchasing—no chair is genuine without it. Our trade-mark is a gold transfer, and is designed to be ornamental.

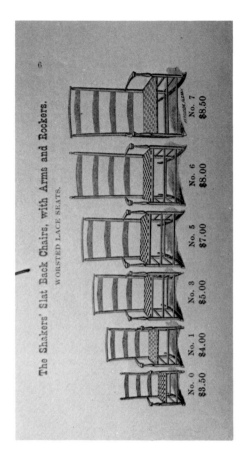

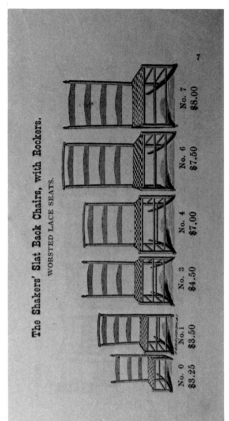

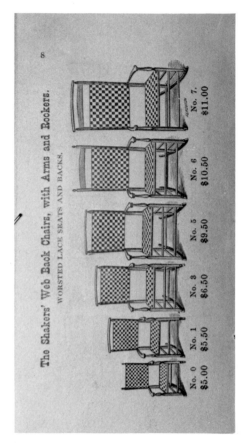

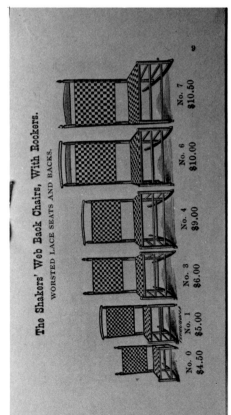

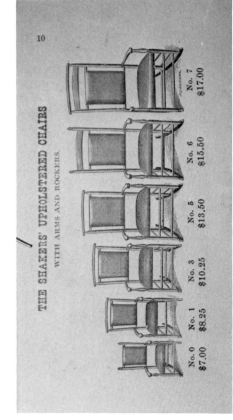

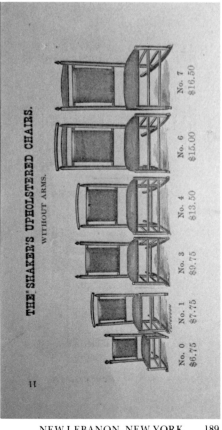

No. 7.   No. 3.

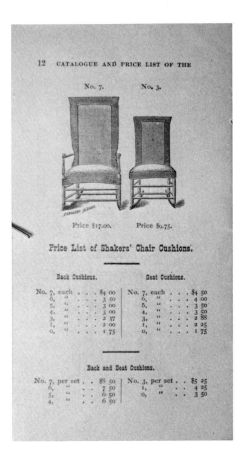

Price $17.00.   Price $9.75.

Price List of Shakers' Chair Cushions.

Back Cushions.		Seat Cushions.	
No. 7, each	$4 00	No. 7, each	$4 50
6, "	3 50	6, "	4 00
5, "	3 00	5, "	3 50
4, "	3 00	4, "	3 50
3, "	2 37	3, "	2 88
1, "	2 00	1, "	2 25
0, "	1 75	0, "	1 75

Back and Seat Cushions.

No. 7, per set	$8 50	No. 3, per set	$5 25
6, "	7 50	1, "	4 25
5, "	6 50	0, "	3 50
4, "	6 50		

We cushion this Foot Bench to match the Cushioned Chairs, in which manner the most of them are sold.

PRICE LIST OF SHAKERS' FOOT BENCHES.

Foot Benches, $1.00; Cushioned, $2.75.
Two-step Benches, $1.50; Cushioned, $3.25.

FLOOR RUGS.

Our Floor Rugs are made of the same material and colors as the cushions. When ordering the Floor Rugs be particular to state the dimensions in length and width; also describe the color of the center and border, if any border is desirable. Our Plush Floor Rugs are sold at the rate of seventy-five cents per square foot.

We also make Wool Rugs and Foot Cushions in the following colors: White, Yellow, Maroon, Blue, Black and Old Gold. Our foot stools are also covered with the above colors of Wool, at same price as with Plush.

☞ We were awarded a Diploma and Medal at the Centennial Exhibition for combining in our chairs, Strength, Sprightliness and Modest Beauty.

Price List of Shakers' Chairs

Worsted Lace Seats.

NO ARMS.   NO ROCKERS.

No. 7,	- - - - - -	$7 50
6,	- - - - - -	7 00
4,	- - - - - -	6 50
3,	- - - - - -	4 00
1,	- - - - - -	3 25
0,	- - - - - -	3 00

Price List of Shakers' Chairs

Worsted Lace Seats and Backs.

NO ARMS.   NO ROCKERS.

No. 7,	- - - - -	$10 00
6,	- - - - -	9 50
4,	- - - - -	8 50
3,	- - - - -	5 50
1,	- - - - -	4 50
0,	- - - - -	4 25

Price Chair Frames.

No 7,	- - - - -	$4 50
6,	- - - - -	4 00
5,	- - - - -	3 50
4,	- - - - -	3 00
3,	- - - - -	2 50
1,	- - - - -	2 00
0,	- - - - -	1 75

Price Rocker Frames

No. 7,	- - - - -	$4 75
6,	- - - - -	4 25
5,	- - - - -	3 75
4,	- - - - -	3 25
3,	- - - - -	2 75
1,	- - - - -	2 25
0,	- - - - -	2 00

Price Arm Frames.

No. 7,	- - - - -	$4 75
6,	- - - - -	4 25
5,	- - - - -	3 75
3,	- - - - -	2 75
1,	- - - - -	2 25
0,	- - - - -	2 00

Price Arm Rocker Frames.

No. 7,	- - - - -	$5 00
6,	- - - - -	4 75
5,	- - - - -	4 50
3,	- - - - -	3 50
1,	- - - - -	2 50
0,	- - - - -	2 25

Dimensions of Shakers' Rocking Chair Seats

NO. OF CHAIR.	WIDTH.	DEPTH.	HEIGHT OF CENTER OF SEAT FROM FLOOR
0	12 in.	10 in.	8½ in.
1	14 "	11½ "	12 "
3	18 "	14½ "	
4	21 "	17½ "	
5	19 "	16½ "	14 "
6	21 "	17½ "	
7	22 "	18½ "	

Height of the Back of Chairs.

NO.	FROM FLOOR.	ABOVE SEAT.
0	23½ in.	16 in.
1	29 "	17½ "
3	35 "	21½ "
4	35 "	22 "
5	28½ "	26 "
6	42½ "	29 "
7	42½ "	29 "

COLORS OF
BRAID AND PLUSH,
Used in our Chairs and Cushions.

Colors of Braid.		Colors of Plush.	
No.		Letter.	
1	Black.	A	Scarlet and Bl'k Stripe.
2	Navy Blue.	B	Blue and Black Stripe.
3	Peacock Blue.	C	Orange and Bl'k Stripe.
4	Light Blue.	D	Blue.
5	Maroon.	E	Black.
6	Pomegranate.	F	Scarlet.
7	Brown.	G	Maroon.
8	Grass Green.	H	Orange.
9	Dark Olive.	I	Peacock Blue.
10	Light Olive.	J	Pomegranate.
11	Old Gold.	K	Olive.
12	Drab.	L	Old Gold.
13	Scarlet.	M	Drab.
14	Orange.	N	Ecrue.

Any two of above colors can be used in combination in Seats and Backs, or in solid colors.

Any two of above colors of Plush can be used in combination or solid colors in cushions.

N. B.—Please use numbers and letters when ordering the colors of braid and plush, and mention which you want for center and border of cushions. The plush cannot be used in combination of colors on the *upholstered* chairs: only one color, except the *A, B* and *C*, which are two colors combined in narrow stripe.

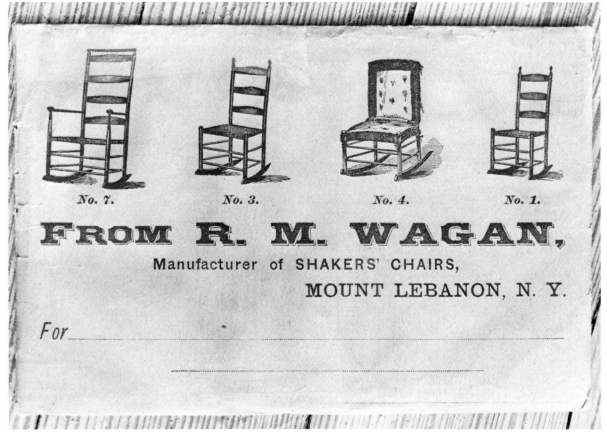

1 Armless rocker, ca.1880-1920. No. 0. R.M. Wagan standard with straight stretchers, dark varnish, and twill tape. (Courtesy of The Shaker Museum, Old Chatham, New York)

2 Armchair, ca.1880-1920. No. 1. R.M. Wagan with tapered front stretchers and straight side stretchers. (Courtesy of The Shaker Museum, Old Chatham, New York)

3 Child with Shaker bonnet seated in No. 0 rocker, date unknown. Size identifiable by single side stretchers. (Courtesy of the Hancock Shaker Village, Inc., Pittsfield, Massachusetts)

4 Rocker, ca.1875. No. 1. Child's. Studio photograph from Lloyd, 44 Third Street, Troy, New York. (Timothy D. Rieman)

1

2

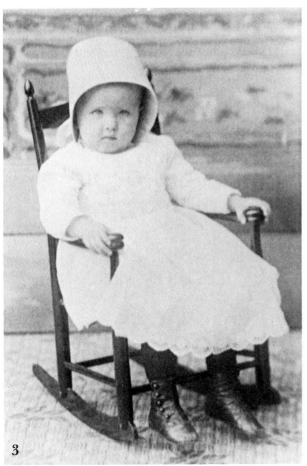

3

4

Armed rocker, ca.1880-1920. No. 6. Tape back. (Courtesy of the Hancock Shaker Village, Inc., Pittsfield, Massachusetts)

Fannie Esterbrook. Photograph by William Teague. ca.1950. (Courtesy of the Hancock Shaker Village, Inc., Pittsfield, Massachusetts)

Armless rocker, ca.1870-75. No. 3. (Courtesy of the Hancock Shaker Village, Inc., Pittsfield, Massachusetts)

Armed rocker, ca.1870-80. (Collection of DeGiorgis and VanAlstyne)

Letter accounting for the chairs given to
the Church Family by the South Family
following the fire at the Church Family
dwelling. (Courtesy, Henry Francis du
Pont Winterthur Museum. The Edward
Deming Andrews Memorial Shaker
Collection)

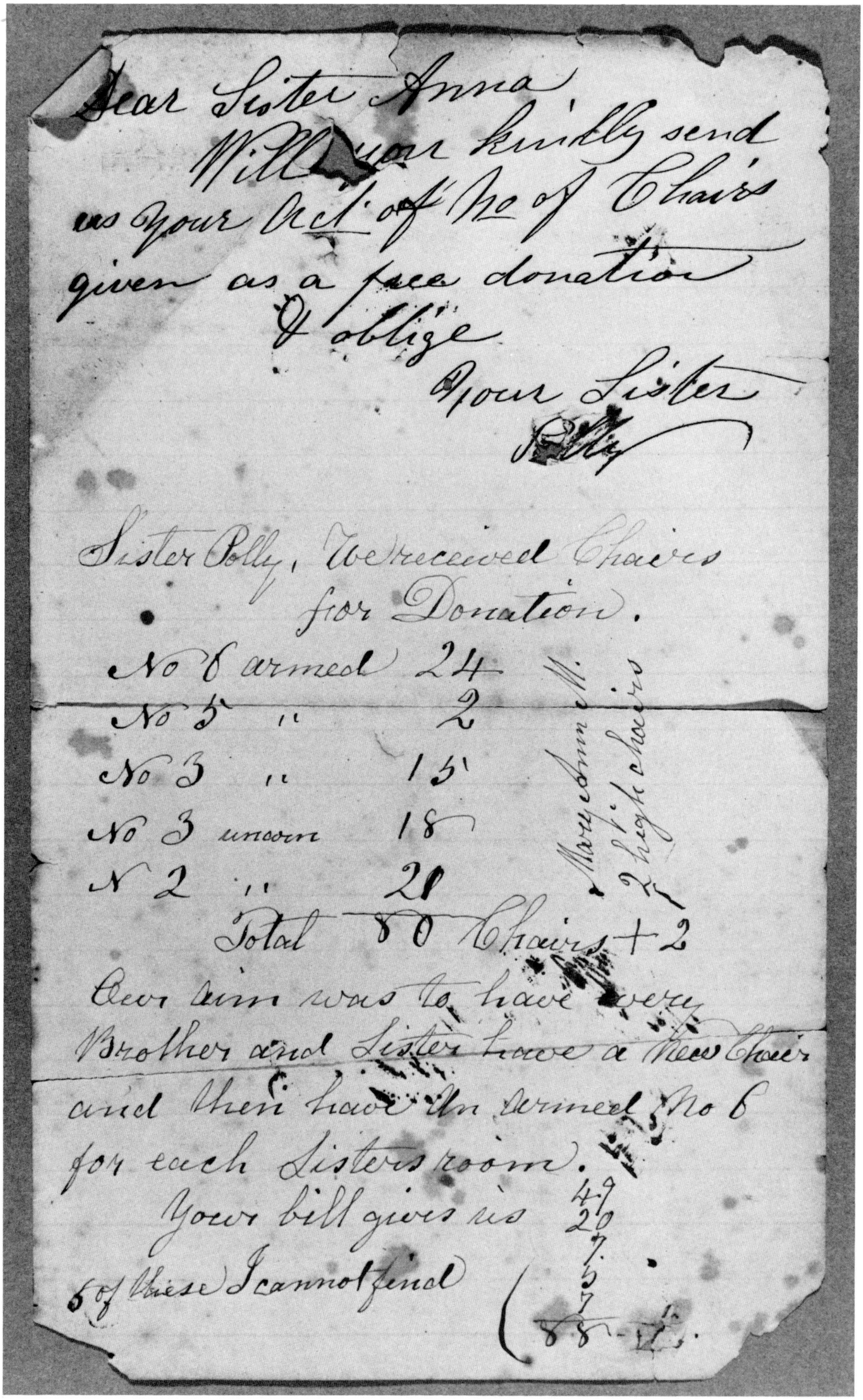

Dear Sister Anna,

Will you kindly send
us your Act off No of Chairs
given as a free donation
& oblige

Your Sister
Polly

Sister Polly, We received Chairs
for Donation.

No 6 armed 24
No 5 " 2
No 3 " 15
No 3 uncom 18
N 2 " 21
Total 80 Chairs + 2

Mary Ann M.
2 high chairs

Our aim was to have every
Brother and Sister have a new Chair
and then have an armed No 6
for each Sisters room.

Your bill gives us   49
                      20
                       7
5 of these I cannot find   5
                            7
                          (88

Child's high chair, ca.1880. Only a small number of these chairs were made. They vary in width and have from one to three slats. (Art Complex Museum of Duxbury)

Armless rocker, ca.1880-1920. No. 4. Two side stretchers removed. The drawer was set on guides fastened to front and rear posts. Black and red paint. (Courtesy of The Shaker Museum, Old Chatham, New York)

Armchair, ca.1880-1900. Unusually deep seat. No. 7 decal on back slat. Seat height — 18½ inches. Probably made as a special order. Original finish. (Courtesy of Richard and Betty Ann Rasso)

Work chair, ca.1870-80. No. 3 stamped on back slat. The rear posts were probably No. 6 rear posts. The tall front posts made specially for this chair. Seat height 21⅞ inches. (Courtesy of The Shaker Museum, Old Chatham, New York)

Side chair, ca.1880-1920. No. 3. Tapered front stretchers and straight side stretchers. (Art Complex Museum of Duxbury)

Side chair. No. 4. Very broad proportions. Very few side chairs of this size were made. (Collection of DeGiorgis and Van Alstyne)

Armed rocker with bar, ca.1880-1900.
(Private Collection)

FILLING CHAIR ORDERS   MT. LEBANON, N.Y.

Splint seat, 1810-1860. The splints were of uniform widths often from ⅜″ to ½″ wide. (Courtesy of the New York State Museum, Albany, New York)

Handwoven tape seat, ca.1840. Many different thread colors were used in this tape. (Courtesy of the New York State Museum, Albany, New York)

Tape seat, ca.1930. Commercial tape. (From the collection of the United Society of Shakers, Sabbathday Lake, Maine)

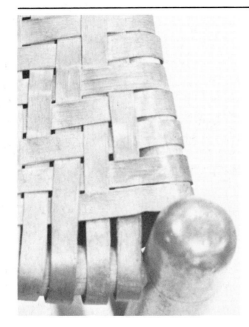

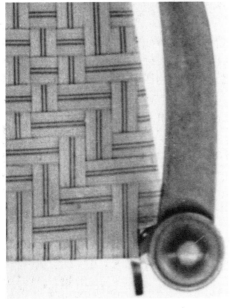

The illustrated catalogues and chair order books offer numerous options available to customers. The chair frames were priced according to size, 0 through 7. This number was impressed into the back of the top slat as well as printed on the trademark transfer. On some later chairs and stools, transfers with the incorrect numbers were used on some products.

Additional costs were listed for web seat or back, arms, rockers, and cushions. The No. 2 size is listed in only earliest catalogues and was not advertised with arms. This was also true of the No. 4. The No. 5 was available only with arms. A close reading, though, of the chair order books indicates that exceptions were made. The option of button join tilts is only listed in the 185- price list but does not appear in later catalogues.

Mahogany was the most common of the finishes provided, with *Cherry, Ebony,* and *White . . . that is the natural color of the maple wood* also available. An occasional order for walnut was also filled. In Brother Henry Blinn's journal of 1872, he writes: *They are all stained in a hot log wood dye which forces the color into the wood. When varnished they are bright red.* Some who visited Sister Lillian Barlow and Brother William Perkins early in this century have related the care and effort that went into the finishing of the chairs. Three or more coats of shellac were applied. Perhaps a better method of finishing was being used than years earlier when an order from the Robert Mitchell Furniture Company in Cincinnati, Ohio, requested on December 5, 1884, *a better stain and finish than last lot for a particular customer.*

As noted in the journal of Brother Benjamin Lyon, the seating material of some early chairs was rush. He recorded on August 23, 1834, that *I go with Garret R. Laromce to Barkers to engague some flags to bottom chares.* Two days later, he went *down to Gilberts to get some flags to bottom chares.* On January 27, 1840, his journal records that *I work some in the shop at spliting out chare splints for Gideon.* Then on February 12, 1840, he worked *some at helping Gideon grind knives to split chare splints.*

Splint was the main seating material of the 1850s. It is mentioned first on the 185- broadside, but is not listed in the catalogues of the 1870s. While less frequently used by that time, an 1873 journal describes Elder Daniel Boler as *splitting chair stuff* for the South Family. Cane, not listed in any of the broadsides or catalogues, was used on some mid-nineteenth century chairs and was purchased from the American Rattan & Reed Mfg. Co. into the 1900s.

The standard seating material of the industry by the 1870s was *web, worsted lace, listing,* or *braid.* Brother Henry DeWitt of New Lebanon designed some of the first tape looms as he mentioned in his journal entry of March, 1833: *I commenced a new kind of business. It was making little spools for to weave tape with.* In 1856, *webbing* was purchased, while *listing* was obtained in September of 1866.

These early tapes were mainly wool. Sometimes linen or cotton threads were mixed with the wool to add stability. Later, tapes used

at the beginning of the twentieth century were cotton and, generally were called webbing. Early tapes were usually woven on two-harness looms used for tabby or plain weave. Patterns were created by the use of color. Four-harness or multi-harness looms were often used in the production of warp-rib weaves.

In 1850, the Sisters of the First Order wove 3,786 yards of tape, according to the yearly report. The 1859 report notes, *810 yards of tape for chairs.* But the following year's account lists $213.22 as expenses for *Chair frames and tape.*

The *Journal kept by the Deaconesses at the Office* of *Work done by the Sisters in the year* gives the division of labor between the orders as well as the amount of production. The Office and First Orders made *51 Chair Mats* in 1841, *50 Shag Chair mats* in 1844, and a like number in 1845. They produced 152 mats or cushions from 1853 through 1860. Another task of the Office Order was the sacking of *chairs for market.* Almost 350 chairs were prepared for shipment in the four years from 1860 to 1864.

The seating or bottoming was done by the Second Order, credited in the Journal with seating 352 chairs from 1859 to 1864, the first year after the South Family assumed the lead for chair production. In that year, $123.50 was paid for chair frames and $125 for tape and hair. Cash received for chairs was $335.50.

The chair order books point out the variety of seating possible: *wide web, All Webs to run Diagonal, Assorted Solid colors, Send some bright Brown, broad Black & Red strip, (1 inch) Webbing laid in squares, Blue, Plum, Blue & Drab,* and *Blue & Drab or Blue and White Web if you can.* The price lists of earlier catalogues offer web and upholstered backs, but illustrations of these do not appear until the Ferguson engravings are used in 1876.

Chair lace was purchased from Horstmann Bro. & Co. of Philadelphia. On November 18, 1885, a check for $769.96 was written to this firm for *Chair Braid.* In a later year, the General Electric Co. in Pittsfield was a source for listing as evidenced by a check written on August 20, 1921, for *1800 yds. 1 in. Brown webbing .7¢.*

Some of the lace received color from the Pittsfield Dye House, which was paid $18.72 on April 11, 1886; but most of it was dyed by the Shakers themselves. They had been using aniline chemical dyes since 1856. These were not as colorfast as the early vegetable dyes, but came in a variety of colors, including orange, scarlet, drab, gold, light and dark olive, green, brown, pomegranate, maroon, light and peacock blue, navy, and black.

Back or seat cushions which could be tied to the rail or around the posts below the pommels were listed in all the broadsides and catalogues. These were of the same material as the upholstered backs and came in the same range of plain colors as the webbing, as well as in scarlet, blue, or orange with a black stripe.

Armed rocker, No. 7 with bar and cushions, 1873. Though the account books show large numbers of cushioned chairs were sold very few exist today. (Courtesy of The Shaker Museum, Old Chatham, N.Y.)

Receipt for the cushioned chair shown above, 1873. Documentation which permits exact dating of this arm style which was made for a short period. (Courtesy of The Shaker Museum, Old Chatham, N.Y.)

" . . . we went over to the South family to see the Elders and Polly Lewis and got some shag yarn for knitting chair cushions, and Eldress Anna has doubled and twisted and already begun to knit three cushions."
October 16, 1869
Journal kept by Giles Avery

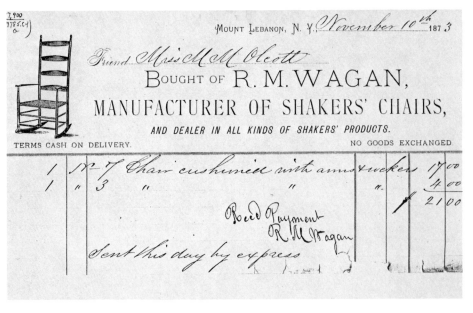

"Library at Arbor Hill" by Walter L. Palmer, 1878. Oil on canvas. Shows the upholstered rocker on opposite page. (Collection Albany Institute of History and Art)

A good description of the making of the plush material is recorded in the Elder Henry Blinn journal:

> *The plush for cushions is made in this building. In one room we found two old men at work in hand looms, weaving this particular cloth. Our guide informed us that they were not Americans. He also informed us that this style of goods cannot be woven by power looms. It is beat up on wire that are grooved. They use only two wires & when the second is secured in its place, they draw a knife across the first wire, in the groove, and then remove it beyond the one already in the loom. Every few minutes they must stop & cut out the wire, which makes the plush. These men weave from three to four yards each day, and are paid fifty cents a yard. One of the men informed me that they usually worked ten hours each day.*

One of these weavers was Emanual Sadilek who was paid $120 on December 23, 1906, for *Weaving Plush, Sisters acct.*

The ten-hour day was standard in the 1880 Census of Manufacturers, along with the average daily wage of $1.75. At this time, six males and one female were employed full time, a contrast with earlier census reports when the factory was dependent upon a seasonally sporadic water supply to generate the needed power. The boiler, engine, and steam power permitted year-round work. The industry was reported as having a capital value of $10,000, as well as values of $5,000 for material and $10,000 in products.

By 1880, the New Lebanon chair business had become well established and the style standardized. This can be seen by the use of duplicating machinery, simplification of style, printing and distribution of catalogues, development of wholesale business, and extensive retail sales throughout the United States and even to England: November 18, 1874—*No. 4 Rocker with all Scarlet Cushions—Securely packed to go to England.*

Comments in the journals attest to the activity and importance of the chair industry as it approaches the end of its first century as a financial source for the United Society of Believers:

> *June 10, 1879—Robert moved the chairs all upstairs to clapboard the room and furnished it up with cushion chairs for a show room, ceiling the room all around.*

> *November 17, 1878—good many chair order comes in.*

> *November 16, 1882—RW has hired another woman from Whitens house to seat chairs.*

> *January 29, 1883—great hurry with orders of chairs.*

> *June 19, 1883—Chair orders keep us more than comfortable.*

Then, on November 29, 1883, Brother Robert Wagan, the most influential leader in the Shaker chair industry, died of pneumonia. The next issuance of a broadside contained an announcement of Brother Robert's death that *The business will be continued, in all its branches under firm name of R.M. Wagan & Co.*

Two months after the death of Brother Robert, Brother William Anderson was moved from the Church Family to the South Family and assumed the leadership of the chair industry. A newspaper account of Brother Robert's death forty years later stated that he *put the chair business on a paying basis as a member of the South colony. He created a nation-wide market for Shaker chairs.* Cancelled checks, order books, and other sources from the first year of operation after the change in leadership provide an illustration of the industrialization, magnitude, and variety of the chair business.

NOTICE TO OUR PATRONS.

———— ❂ ————

The sudden decease of our friend and Brother, R. M. WAGAN, may have caused some little delay in filling your orders and due correspondence, which we very much regret, and we hope in the future to avoid all such delays.

Thankful for your past favors we most earnestly solicit a continuance of the same.

The business will be continued in all its branches under firm name of

R. M. WAGAN & CO.,
MOUNT LEBANON,
COL. CO., N. Y.

JAN. 16, 1884.

Portrait of Brother William Anderson, date unknown. Little documentation exists relating Brother William's leadership in the chair industry over the decades following the death of Brother Robert Wagan. (Courtesy of Jerry Grant)

In 1884, some of the materials used in the manufacturing of the chairs was being purchased from outside companies. Chair rounds were obtained from D. C. Jones & Sons of Berlin, New York, who were paid $50 on September 13 for 7,000 rounds. *Felt for chair cushions* was purchased for $40.32 (cash) for Sister Polly Lewis from H. D. Ostermoor & Son of New York City, while *1 Bale of Bats* for filler in the seats was obtained from W. M. Whitney & Co. of Albany for $7.50. As mentioned earlier, the chair lace came from Horstmann Bro. & Co., to whom checks totaling $1,039.53 were written during the year. Two barrels of wood stain were received from the Bridgeport Wood Furnishing Co. for $76.20 and five gallons of *oil finish shellac* came from the Glidden W. Jay & Co. of Boston for $7.00. Screws for the rockers, 200 gross of 1¼ inches, were purchased for $28 from E. Williams of Pittsfield.

In 1885, John Feathers of Berlin, New York, was a major provider of chair parts as evidenced by a check written on April 10 for $283.50 for *40,500 chair rounds*. Two years later, W. J. Cowee, also of Berlin, was receiving payment for chair parts.

Brick and mason repairs were done on the chair factory in that same year and N. Dodge of Pittsfield received $111.73 for the work. A new steam boiler and fixtures were purchased for $396.78 in September of 1886. H. S. Russell of Pittsfield was the supplier, while Robbins, Gamwell & Co. of the same city received a check of $55.90 for *piping & fixtures for factory*.

The catalogues were printed by Weed, Parsons & Co., which also printed three-colored illustrations of upholstery that were pasted into the catalogues. *Our upholstered chairs differ very materially from our cushioned chairs. The frame of the back is constructed differently, and the cushions are stationary, being fastened to the chair.*

Even though production had become standardized, considerable variety was possible. The chair frames in eight different sizes were available with pommels or cushion bars. Each of these could be ordered with or without rockers, and with (except No. 2 and 4) or without (except No. 5) arms in the four different finishes. Choices were available among the backs (slat, web, upholstered, web with slat) and seats (web, upholstered) in a variety of widths of tapes or types of upholstering. Twenty-one different colors were listed for the upholstery, although many more were probably used over the years. Finally, the customer could add seat and back cushions which were fastened to the chair by strings.

While the catalogues listed hundreds of possible combinations, the Shakers filled special requests that were not offered in the catalogues. Such special requests might refer to the need for specific measurements or a desire to match an earlier style. The 1884-1885 chair order book notes some of these:

June—Geo. H. Tucker—No. 5-A—old style
August—#5—new style frame
January—The chairs to have the old fashioned straight backs as made originally.
September—1 set chair cushions in solid maroon . . .

February—1-A. Seat 1 in. higher than regular
November—No. 6-A—Sp. Pad for an invalid
November—Box-shape Cushion, Lamb-skin top
December—Lounge Cushion, Angora
March—Cushions for Swiss rocker as per pattern
November—Height of this last chair from floor—14 inc. in front, 12 inc. at back, solid maroon . . .
September—The seat to be 20" from the floor or 4" more than the . . . frame old cushion chair
November—All to have seats 17 in. from floor, Soon as possible.
March—the seat 3 in. higher than regular make
November—High Chair, bar top, web back, maroon.
October—armless No. 5
July—No 2—seat to be 12. in from rocker as a No 2.
August—No 3 . . . seat to be 12½ in. from center of rocker to seat. Wanted soon.
February—Seat 1 in. higher than regular

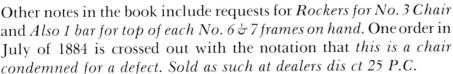

Other notes in the book include requests for *Rockers for No. 3 Chair* and *Also 1 bar for top of each No. 6 & 7 frames on hand.* One order in July of 1884 is crossed out with the notation that *this is a chair condemned for a defect. Sold as such at dealers dis ct 25 P.C.*

Chair orders were filled during the year for such wholesale businesses as A.H. Davenport of Boston, King and Elder of Indianapolis, Indiana, and the Phoenix Furniture Co. of Grand Rapids, Michigan. In Philadelphia, the following stores received orders: J. Wanamaker, Jos. Page, Sharpless & Sons, Horstman Bros. & Co., Howard & Crawford, and John H. Sanderson. The list of companies in New York City includes Charles Jones, Lewis & Conger, Banner & Moore, Doremus & Corbett, DeGraff & Taylor, A. G. Newman, The John Shillito Co., Herts Brothers, Warren Ward & Co., Herman Friend, Wm. Zepp, Brunner & Moore, Newman & Co., R. J. Bloomer, Nicholas Power, Lewis P. Tibbals, and Charles Brothers. One chair bears the label of the Scharles & Sons Co., as well as that of the Shakers. Orders from the R. J. Bloomer firm stand out because of the sizable quantities of No. 0's: for example, 25 were ordered on October 31, 25 on November 15, and another 40 two days later on November 16. In the same period, the company ordered only fifteen other chairs with ten of these being No. 1's.

One particular order is worthy of note because of its size: J. E. Kingsley and Co. placed an order for H.H. Houston, to be used in his new Wissahicon Hotel in Chestnut Hill, Pennsylvania. Two-hundred-and-fifty No. 3 and No. 5 chairs were *To be completed and shipped by May 10.* The order was received on March 29 and the chairs shipped on May 9.

A tabulation of the orders recorded in the chair order book from
February 1884 through March 1885 shows the following distribution:

Size	Side	Armed	Armless Rocker	Armed Rocker
0	1	12	19	291
1	3	14	36	95
2	7	—	92	48
3	33	9	636	218
4	20	3	199	4
5	—	128	15	349
6	—	9	29	340
7	—	30	25	303
Total	64	205	1051	1596

The approximate breakdown on back styles is web—39 percent, slat—44 percent, upholstered—8 percent, cushion—9 percent. These figures, taken from the order book, do not include chairs sold from the store in the Shaker Village. Nor do they adequately account for general orders like that of John Wanamaker on October 6: *6 Chairs uphd assorted in size and color.*

Side chair, 1887. A variation of the South Family's No. 3 chair made for use in the Meeting House. Rectangular seat stretchers doweled into the posts and fitted with a plywood seat. (Americana Antiques)

One variation of the production chairs that appears to have been made exclusively for use within the Shaker community was a side chair for the New Lebanon meeting house. Bearing the No. 3 imprint on the back of the top slat, these were constructed with square seat rails to support the flat punched plywood seats. A check dated September 6, 1887, for $33.68 was written for *chair seats, Meeting House* and indicates Frost & Peterson of New York was the source. The New Lebanon Sisters Journal for 1887 recorded: *We have a new arrangement for the Meeting House, instead of benches, we have Chairs made at (the) South Family, 4 Chairs are fastened together.* These chairs have screw holes on the inside of the rear posts, where horizontal boards had at one time held four chairs together.

As the second century of chair production at New Lebanon began, its focus continued to expand from that of meeting primarily the needs of its own Society to that of being deeply involved in the manufacturing and selling of its wares to the world. Checks written for *labor at the factory* increased in number, and shipments were made with greater regularity to sales centers. An 1885-1886 book for the Boston & Albany Railroad records the sending of chairs to such places as Henry A. Turner & Co. of Boston, W. C. Moses & Sons of Washington, D.C., Potter & Co. of Providence, Rhode Island, Gorton & McCabe of Rochester, New York, Oliver McClintock & Co. of Pittsburg, The Gayton Furniture Co. of Cleveland, and Troxel Brothers of Burlington, Iowa. Scattered amidst these company names are those of individuals from Philadelphia to Chicago to Salt Lake City.

The largest recipient listed in the shipping book is Marshall Field & Co., a Chicago firm that printed its own catalogue of Shaker chairs shortly after the turn of the century. On December 28, 1894, an order of 23 chairs was shipped to Marshall Field & Co. On February 26 of the following year, another 37 chairs were sent. Then, on April 5, along with 3 chairs, 2 settees are listed. Another 13 chairs and 1 settee followed two weeks later. While settees are today considered among the rare forms originating from the South Family's chair factory, these references and the copy in the July, 1895, *Manifesto* would indicate production and availability of this form to the public:

Settee, ca. 1890. An unusual variation made at the New Lebanon factory, this settee made use of chair side stretchers, posts and arms with the addition of specially made long stretchers between pairs of front and back posts. Order books record several sales. (The Sherman Collection)

Boston & Albany RR receipt for the shipment of chairs and settees to the Marshall Field & Co., 1895. Several freight receipt books exist listing a variety of destinations. (Courtesy, Henry Francis duPont Winterthur Museum, The Edward Deming Andrews Memorial Shaker Collection, No. SA 934)

There continues a constant demand for the famous Shaker chairs, sofas, footrests, and numerous other articles . . . We are quite positive that the South Family at Mount Lebanon is the champion chair maker of the world. The work is of the very best and it is known that

> *They're useful---ornamental.*
> *Two grand principals combined.*
> *You may search the whole world over,*
> *Nor better chairs you'll find.*
> *Then their sofas and their footrests*
> *Are the best the world can give;*
> *Do not try to find their equal,*
> *For you cannot while you live.*

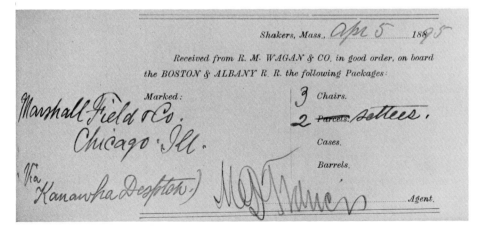

CATALOGUE

OF

SHAKERS' CHAIRS

MADE BY THE

SOCIETY OF SHAKERS

AT

MOUNT LEBANON, N. Y.

THIS is the only chair manufactory in existence which is owned and operated by the Shakers. No expense or labor is spared in producing a perfect article, which combines all the advantages of durability, simplicity and lightness. The frames are made of mountain maple finished in natural color or to imitate dark mahogany and are either for chairs or rockers.

MARSHALL FIELD & CO.,

RETAIL UPHOLSTERY DEPT.

STATE & WASHINGTON STS., CHICAGO.

STYLES OF ROCKERS.

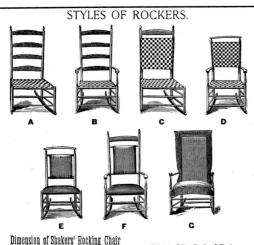

A   B   C   D

E   F   G

Dimension of Shakers' Rocking Chair Seats.

SIZE NO.	WIDTH	DEPTH	HEIGHT OF CENTER OF SEAT FROM FLOOR
1	14 in	11½ in	12 in
3	18 "	14½ "	
4	21 "	17½ "	14 "
5	19 "	16½ "	
7	22 "	18½ "	

Height of the Back of Chairs.

SIZE NO.	FROM FLOOR	ABOVE SEAT
1	29 in	17½ in
3	35 "	21½ "
4	35 "	22 "
5	38½ "	26 "
7	42½ "	29 "

COLORS OF BRAID.

No.	
1	Black.
2	Navy Blue.
3	Peacock Blue.
4	Light Blue.
5	Maroon.
6	Pomegranate.
7	Brown.
8	Grass Green.
9	Dark Olive.
10	Light Olive.
11	Old Gold.
12	Drab.
13	Scarlet.
14	Orange.

Any two of above colors can be used in combination in Seats and Backs, or in solid colors.

COLORS OF PLUSH.

Letter	
A	Scarlet and Black Stripe.
B	Blue and Black Stripe.
C	Orange and Black Stripe.
D	Blue.
E	Black.
F	Scarlet.
G	Maroon.
H	Orange.
I	Peacock Blue.
J	Pomegranate.
K	Olive.
L	Old Gold.
M	Drab.
N	Ecru.

Any two of above colors of Plush can be used in combination or solid colors in cushions.

N. B.—Please use numbers and letters when ordering the colors of braid and plush, and mention which you want for center and border of cushions. The plush cannot be used in combination of colors on the *upholstered* chairs; only one color, except the *A*, *B* and *C*, which are two colors combined in narrow stripe.

PRICE LIST

	SIZE No.	1	3	4	5	7
Style A. Mahogany Rocker		$4.25	$5.25	$8.00	——	$9.50
OA. Maple "						
AA. Mahogany Chair		3.75	4.50	7.50	——	9.00
OAA. Maple "						
B. Mahogany Rocker		4.50	5.75	——	$8.00	9.50
OB. Maple "						
BB. Mahogany Chair		4.00	5.25	——	7.50	9.00
OBB. Maple "						
C. Mahogany Rocker		6.00	7.00	10.00	——	12.00
OC. Maple "						
CC. Mahogany Chair		5.25	6.00	9.50	——	11.25
OCC. Maple "						
D. Mahogany Rocker		6.00	7.50	——	11.00	12.50
OD. Maple "						
DD. Mahogany Chair		5.75	7.00	——	10.00	12.00
ODD. Maple "						
E. Mahogany Rocker		9.00	11.50	——	14.50	18.00
OE. Maple "						
EE. Mahogany Chair		9.00	11.00	——	14.00	17.50
OEE. Maple "						
F. Mahogany Rocker		9.50	12.00	——	15.00	18.50
OF. Maple "						
FF. Mahogany Chair		9.50	11.50	——	14.75	18.00
OFF. Maple "						
G. Mahogany Rocker		9.50	12.00	——	15.00	18.50
OG. Maple "						
GG. Mahogany Chair		9.50	11.50	——	14.75	18.00
OGG. Maple "						

As indicated by some checks written to Brother Henry G. Green of Alfred, Maine, not all distribution was through large city firms. A December 7, 1898, entry lists $67.75 paid to the Shaker elder *On chairs sold at the Mts.* On November 4, 1908, a check was written for *Disct. on chairs sold,* and another, December 25, 1909, for $15.87, has the notation *Commission on Chairs sold.*

In addition to sales through the catalogues and wholesale outlets, a retail store was maintained in the Shaker Village. This is often referred to in the chair order books and is mentioned in the catalogues:

> *We have a store in the south end of the street or village where the chairs are made, and where a full assortment of our chairs and all other goods of our manufacture are kept for sale, and where a great many travelers and visitors from all parts of the country and the world invariably call and see something which is purchased and taken away with them, the most desireable of them all being our chairs.*

"A short time since we heard a lady ask her companion if she had any of the Shakers' chairs in her house. She replied, "Certainly I have, and I would go without bread in my family before I would dispose with my pretty Shakers' chairs."
Illustrated Catalogue and Price List of the Shakers' Chairs, 1874

"We have a store in the south end of the street or village where the chairs are made, and where a full assortment of our chairs and all other goods of our manufacture are kept for sale, and where a great many travelers and visitors from all parts of the country & the world invariably call and see something which is purchased and taken away with them, the most desireable of them all being our chairs."
Illustrated Catalogue and Price List of the Shakers' Chairs, 1874

SOUTH FAMILY SHAKER CHAIR STORE MT LEBANON N.Y.

The absence of documents relating to the chair industry in the first two decades of the twentieth century suggests a decline in manufacturing, although the March 4, 1909, check written to Palm Fechteler & Co. for *10,000 chair Trade marks* indicates an intention to continue production. A statement in the *Springfield Republican* of December 30, 1923, following the destruction of the chair factory by fire, offers a little insight into this period:

For more than 80 years Shaker chairs were made in the ancient stone shop, then the industry lapsed until a few years ago when it was revived through the enterprise of Eldress Egelson. It had just gotten onto a good paying basis again.

The fire of December 28, 1923, destroyed the five-story stone structure that had been used as a chair factory. The following is the account that appeared in *the Berkshire Evening Eagle* the next day:

A fire which lighted up the country for miles around last night, burned four buildings belonging to the Second Family of the Shaker community in Mount Lebanon, N.Y. . . . The last of the four buildings burned was a five-story chair factory made of stone, built in 1800, the center of the Shaker chair manufacturing industry of the United States. . . . The fire started when Elder Pick was pouring gasoline from a tank into a small can in the grain building for the use of his automobile. A lighted lantern which was close by ignited the fumes of the gasoline and caused an explosion . . . The flames quickly caught on the inflammable materials in that part of the building. A strong wind was blowing from the west and little could be done to stop the progress of the flames . . . For a time it was thought that the stone factory could be saved. Eldress Margaret Eggleston, head of the women of the family, organized a bucket brigade which effectively saved two other buildings . . . .The Shaker creamery in the factory building was destroyed, as were thousands of dollars worth of the quaint Shaker chairs and much valuable lumber . . .

Portrait of Sister Margaret Egelson who was mentioned in newspaper article. (Courtesy of the Shaker Library, The United Society of Shakers, Sabbathday Lake, Maine)

Sister Lillian Barlow and Brother William Perkins, ca. 1935. Probably the primary members involved in the manufacture of chairs in the twentieth century. (Courtesy of Richard and Betty Ann Rasso)

On the day following the 1923 destruction of the chair factory, the *Springfield Republican* printed an article on the fire with the headline that the *Shakers Will Keep Business—Will Restore Chair-Making Plant at Mt. Lebanon in Another Building.*

The second family of Shakers at Mt. Lebanon comprising six members is not disheartened by the fire which destroyed four large buildings including its only industry on Friday night and is arranging to restore its chair-making plant in another structure. The prime mover in this project is the energetic and intrepid elderess, Miss Margaret Egelson, who will be 80 on June 17 and who has been with the Mount Lebanon Shakers for 68 years. She is being assisted by Sister Lillian Barlow and Brother William H. Perkins, the latter of whom had been superintendent of the chair and woodworking shop for about 10 years . . . In recent years he had installed over $10,000 worth of machinery on the third floor of the factory. In the building also were stored Shaker antiques including much furniture of great value, all of which was destroyed . . . Hundreds of visitors within a radius of 25 miles visited the ruins today. The great stone shop building, five stories high, windowless and roofless stood out like a specter on the landscape. It was built in 1826, all the stone being laid by Shaker artisans and like all Shaker property in good repair.

Although there were several checks written to Warren Fowler of West Lebanon, New York, for *Insurance on chair factory,* the policy must have lapsed. The newspaper account estimated the loss at $50,000 and stated that it was uninsured. *Walter Shapard, who makes his home with the North Family but is the head of all the Shakers of the country . . . said that the loss was a heavy one because of the valuable machinery . . .* and *that the buildings would not be rebuilt, as the Second family still had four or five buildings which were adequate for its needs.*

The Shaker chair industry had been located in various buildings throughout history. One was destroyed by flood in 1814. Another is mentioned as having been constructed in the 1820s. Then on October 15, 1855, some of the brothers *went to help raise a Chair factory frame 2nd F(amily).* Upon the completion of the new one for the South Family, Brother Robert Wagan *is haven the old chair factory torn down.* On April 3, 1876, *Some of the Brethren went to the old factory to take the frame down.* Throughout the changes of leadership and location, the chair business at New Lebanon continued.

In his sixties by the time of the fire, Brother William Perkins reestablished the chair business. Upon his death, March 13, 1934, the *Berkshire Eagle* said of him:

After the conflagration he installed a smaller plant in one of the neighboring wooden structures, a stone's throw from the charred walls of the old factory. Shaker chairs and other articles by the thousands were turned out under his skillful direction. He had charge of building the chair frames while Sister Sarah Collins at the South Family wove the seats.

Sister Sarah Collins, herself amost seventy years old at the time of the fire, reflected upon the experience when she wrote to a friend on October 3, 1924:

> *Your letter received I have been trying to hurry about the chairs but cannot get hold of the frames for some time yet. So much destroyed by the fire caused the delay. We now have a fine shop but little parts. Gone and replacing some.*
>
> *This has been the greatest trial of my life and could have been avoided.*

A letter addressed to H. H. Ballard was written two weeks later, October 21, and expressed the feelings of joy felt by Brother William in having *a fine shop.* Chairs were once again being produced.

> *. . . I know that you have a kindly feeling towards the Shakers and I feel sure also that you will be glad to know that we have almost entirely renewed our chair shop, and that we are now earning in part. Come over and see the miracle of materialized prayer combined with faith in God and man.*

During the time of reconstruction, the filling of orders for chairs had to be postponed. When production started again, the simpler style of the web back appears to have been made while proper machinery was obtained for the shaping and forming of the back slats. Sister Sarah responded in November of 1925 to one request:

> *Your letter should have been answered sooner. We answer a great many at once, but are not always sure about when we can fill orders . . . The tools for making the slat chairs we have now and I have been talking it up to our Brothers. They have been busy all summer on the web back chairs so many old orders on hand for them I hope soon to get the chairs so that they can be seated. We are having some stools and low back chairs seated in reed they are firm and good ..The new slat back chairs (and) side chairs we find will be higher in price will do our best.*

The rebuilding of the chair factory, purchasing of new equipment, and the advancing years of the makers resulted in significant changes in the design of the chairs produced by the South Family after 1923. The photographs taken by William F. Winter in the late 1920s or early 1930s show numerous machines for drilling and slotting, as well as lathes for turning the pommels by hand. Although lathes for partially turning chair posts are in the photograph, those used for turning entire posts in the large quantities required by the market are absent.

The lack of proper equipment and the small work force point out the Shaker's need to depend ever more strongly upon other manufacturers for much of their materials. Remaining crates of chair arms like those found on the products of this period bear labels of The Readsboro Chair Company of Readsboro, Vermont, while bundles of rounds (stretchers) carry the shipping tags of the Mason

Shipping label, ca. 1920. The Parker and Palmer Co. was the probable source for dowels used for posts in many twentieth century Shaker chairs. (Courtesy of The Shaker Museum, Old Chatham, N.Y.)

Armchairs, ca. 1930. Though the form is similar to earlier chairs, many details were changed when new machinery and jigs were developed. The pommels, back slats, tenon caps, and vase turnings—virtually all the chair parts—were redesigned. The chairs were still identifiable as Shaker and often labeled with the R.M. Wagan decal. (The Art Complex Museum of Duxbury)

Pommel and post, ca. 1930. The Shakers purchased partially turned posts from which they finished the pommel turnings. (From the Collection of the United Society of Shakers, Sabbathday Lake, Maine)

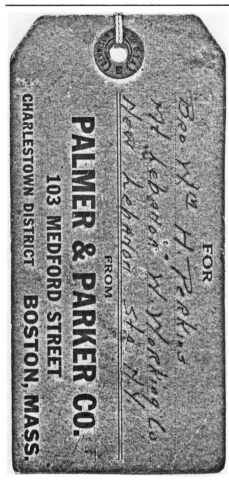

Toy and Novelty Company. Cases of dowels for posts are marked with the name of the Parker and Palmer Company of Tewksbury, Massachusetts.

The changes in design with these new parts are obvious in comparison to corresponding elements of the *standard* R. M. Wagan chairs. These chairs are barren expressions compared to earlier days when form and function were finely intermeshed. Uniformly thick, the arms no longer show projections at the wrists and elbows but have an unbroken movement from post to post that is reminiscent of the earliest production arms. The tenon caps are broader—usually extending beyond the width of the arm—and flatter than the more rounded examples of the late nineteenth century. The posts are heavier in appearance and many of the chairs have all the stretchers made with turned dowels, which show no variance in diameter throughout their length, although some chairs retained front stretchers with tapering on the ends. Using purchased dowels that had been turned to size for the posts, the Shakers or their employees simply turned the pommels on one end and, sometimes, a minimal taper on the other. The accompanying photograph illustrates a turned pommel next to purchased dowels, the stock from which the posts were produced. A few tall five-slat armchairs point out the limitations in the length of the stock as well as the machinery. These chairs will occasionally have the pommels turned separately and then dowelled into the top of the rear posts.

Second Family chair factory. Photograph 1920-40. This is the building referred to in the March 13, 1934, "Berkshire Eagle" article "where the Second family rebuilt the Shaker chair industry." (Courtesy of The Shaker Museum, Old Chatham, N.Y.)

Workroom used by Sister Sarah Collins for taping chairs. See post card view p. 228. (Courtesy of The Shaker Museum, Old Chatham, N.Y.)

Storage room, ca. 1930. Unfinished chair frames. (Courtesy of The Shaker Museum, Old Chatham, N.Y.)

Armless rocker, ca. 1930. The most noticeable changes between this and chairs made at the turn of the century are the presence of straight back posts, less sharply turned pommels, and straight front and side stretchers. (Collection of DeGiorgis and VanAlystene)

Armchair, ca. 1930. Long pommels on straight back posts, broad crescent shaped arms, and flattened tenon caps date this chair after the 1923 fire. (The Art Complex Museum of Duxbury)

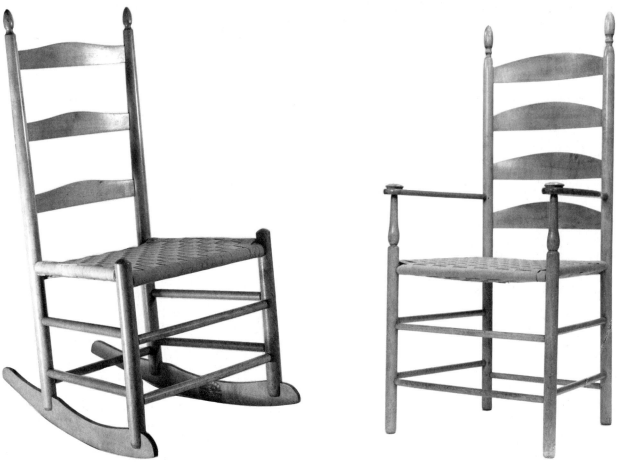

Business card of Brother William Perkins, ca.1930. (Private Collection)

Side chair, ca.1930. This stocky chair uses posts which were partially turned when purchased by the Shakers. Many of these chairs with their heavy posts and straight stretchers have the decal. (The Art Complex Museum of Duxbury)

Armless rocker, ca.1930. Tall posts similar to those used on armchairs. High seat. Very heavy dark varnish. (Courtesy of The Shaker Museum, Old Chatham, New York)

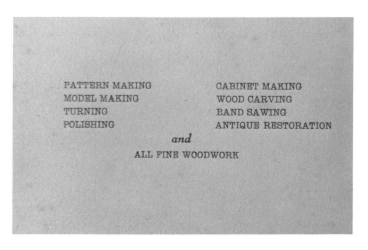

TELEPHONE 132-F4 WEST LEBANON

THE MOUNT LEBANON WOODWORKING CO.

SECOND FAMILY SHAKERS

MOUNT LEBANON, NEW YORK

BROTHER WM. H. PERKINS
REPRESENTATIVE   (OVER

PATTERN MAKING   CABINET MAKING
MODEL MAKING   WOOD CARVING
TURNING   BAND SAWING
POLISHING   ANTIQUE RESTORATION
                    and
        ALL FINE WOODWORK

Armed rocker, 1929. Reminiscent of earlier mushroom post rockers. Back slats similar to R.M. Wagan chairs. Posts do not have scribe marks and are minimally tapered above the seat. Arms are uniform in thickness and fitted with wide flat tenon caps that extend beyond the width of the arms. On the back of slats is written: *"The Ella Bruce Malcom Chair. 1929. Second Family Shakers. Mount Lebanon, N.Y. Lillian Barlow, Wm. H. Perkins. Gods Chosen Few Incarnate in order to Heal."* (Art Complex Museum of Duxbury)

Lillian Barlow in Second Family chair factory, ca.1930. Photographs by Baldwin. Unassembled chair parts in these photographs help to date chairs made in this period. (Courtesy of the New York State Museum, Albany, New York)

One particular variation of the turned pommel on chairs produced from the commercial stock used for posts in the years following the fire is clearly seen in the photograph of Sister Lillian Barlow.

"Sister Lillian Barlow . . . was busy with cooking, canning, gardening, or sewing (she was an accomplished seamstress), but devoted most of her time to making chairs in a barn-like building near the family dwelling. One was almost sure to find her somewhere in the large noisy chair room cluttered with lathes, sanding machines, steam racks and all the accourterments of the industry. Though only one machine might be in use, generally several were operating, the worn leather belts flapping and whirling as they revolved on the pulleys of the overhead shafts. . . . They were always cordial, but the work never stopped and one had to shout to be heard above the din of the belts and wheels, and the chisels biting into the maple chair posts. There was seldom time to sit down and talk. . . . Lillian was loath to part with anything except the chairs she was making, these and her flowers, or her asparagus, or sometimes old books and manuscripts. She had a strong sentimental attachment to any piece of Shaker workmanship. . . . "

Fruits of the Shaker Tree of Life:
Memoirs by Edward Deming Andrews and
Faith Andrews
The Berkshire Traveller Press
(Stockbridge, Mass.: 1975)

"Most of our visitors these days are antique collectors, and all they're interested in is buying up what little fine old handsome furniture we have left. Why, those people would grab the chairs right out from under us if we'd let them. Our furniture is very fashionable all of a sudden. You know, I understand it's called modernistic..."
Jenny Wells 1947

Several low-back chairs were introduced in the last twenty years of Shaker chair production. Often called dressing chairs, there were three variations: one with spherically shaped pommels and horizontal rods or dowels where the back slats normally were; a similar design using standard production back slats; and an example with the top slat resembling a Shaker wooden clothes hanger, which is inserted from the top into slots cut into the posts. The first two often had the trademark decalcomanias.

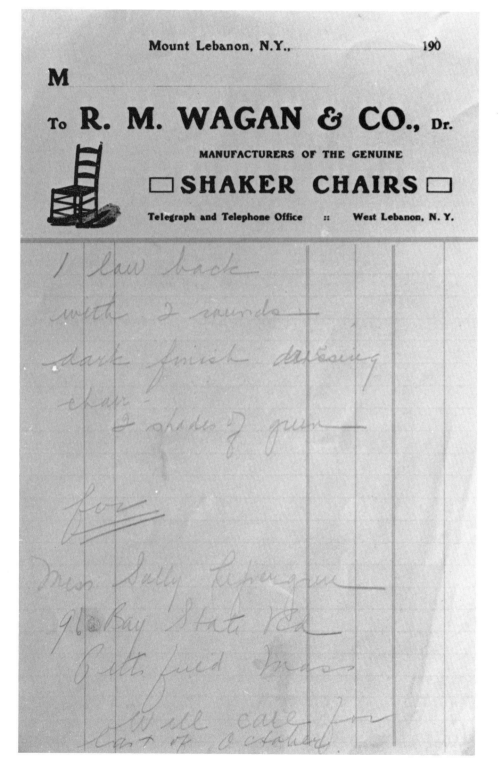

GENUINE SHAKER WORK

Lillian Barlow
Wm. H. Perkins.

Mount Lebanon, New York
October 29 — 1902.

When Brother William Perkins died on March 15, 1934, the business was left in the care of Sisters Sarah Collins and Lillian Barlow.

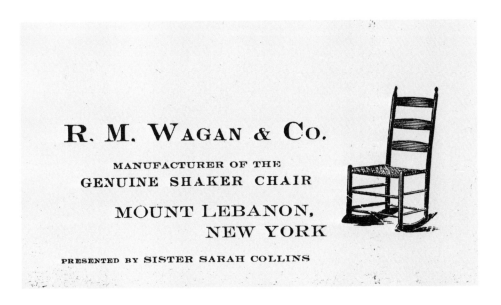

R. M. WAGAN & CO.

MANUFACTURER OF THE
GENUINE SHAKER CHAIR

MOUNT LEBANON,
NEW YORK

PRESENTED BY SISTER SARAH COLLINS

A visit to Sister Sarah and the once thriving industry was described in the August 13, 1933, edition of the *Berkshire Evening Eagle:*

> *Sister Sarah may be found any day at almost any hour seating or refinishing chairs. The building where the shop is located on the second floor, originally contained the laundry. When the family was large, laundry work was done on a huge scale. On the first floor the large boilers and tubs still remain, now used for staining chairs. . . The weaving room is still used by a man who assists sister Sarah, weaving carpets and covers for stools . . .*

> *The chairs on which Sister Sarah works are sent to the ends of the earth. Last year she had an order from Syria, and every week*

orders come in from all over the country. The woodwork is done by the Second Family, who send the chairs to her to be finished and sold. She told of two chairs that had recently returned for reseating which had been made 60 years ago. She knows all the types and can tell who made each chair and when it was made. She does a large business in reseating and refinishing old chairs, for they were made so well that they never wear out, and with a new seat, and perhaps a coat of shellac, they are as good as new.

And now that the old family property has been put on the market, even though a sale is not imminent, Sister Sarah does not relish the idea of stopping work on her chairs. With the hands of an artist she weaves the tape in making the seats and uses shellac in touching up the woodwork of some of them.

I hope I don't have to stop, she said.

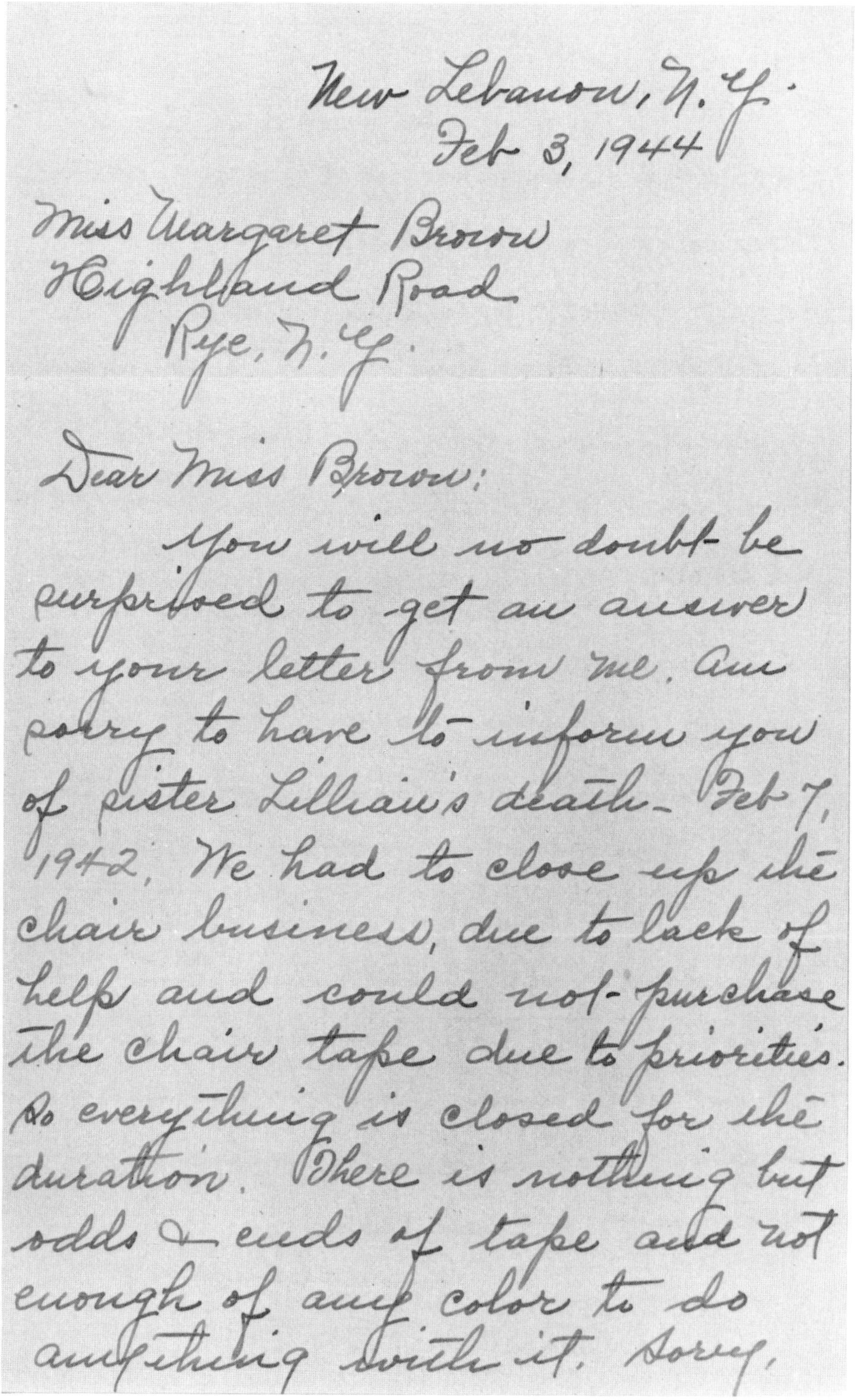

New Lebanon, N. Y.
Feb 3, 1944

Miss Margaret Brown
Highland Road,
Rye, N. Y.

Dear Miss Brown:

You will no doubt be surprised to get an answer to your letter from me. Am sorry to have to inform you of sister Lillian's death — Feb 7, 1942, We had to close up the chair business, due to lack of help and could not purchase the chair tape due to priorities. So everything is closed for the duration. There is nothing but odds & ends of tape and not enough of any color to do anything with it. Sorry, but the wining of this war comes first, and I hope it dont last much longer. What a terrible thing war is, and in these days of civilization it is all the more shameful.

Sister Sarah Collins, is almost 89 yrs old, she is busy on her rugs, but she is getting quite confused and forgetful. She is a dear, never complains of anything. She dont do any writing, her hands are too crippled up from all the chairs she has seated. Thanking you for writing, Jemima,

Respectfully,
Frances Hall.

   The death of Sister Lillian brought to an end more than a century and a half of chairmaking among the Shakers. The last participant in the once-thriving industry was Sister Sarah who had seated the chairs and kept the store. She died in 1947.

APPENDIX:
THE IMITATORS— Non-Shaker Chairs

THE IMITATORS—Non-Shaker Chairs

1

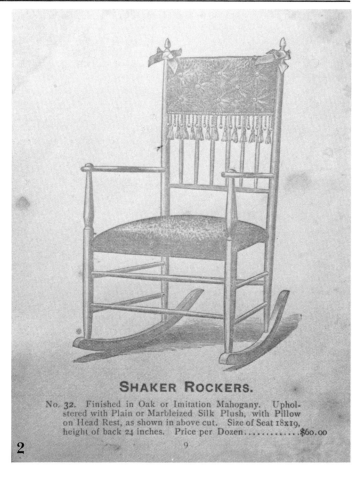

SHAKER ROCKERS.

No. 32. Finished in Oak or Imitation Mahogany. Upholstered with Plain or Marbleized Silk Plush, with Pillow on Head Rest, as shown in above cut. Size of Seat 18x19, height of back 24 inches. Price per Dozen.............$60.00

2

9

3

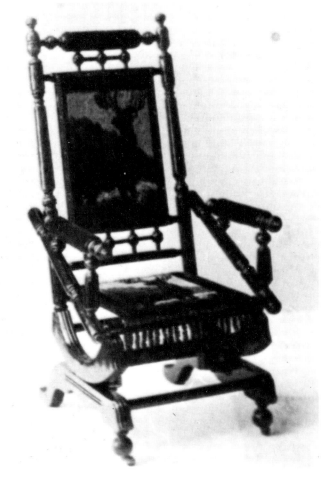

4

THE IMITATORS

. . . We would also call the attention of the public to the fact that there is no other chair manufactory which is owned and operated by the Shakers except the one which is now in operation and owned and operated by the Society of Shakers at Mount Lebanon, Columbia Co. N.Y. We deem it a duty we owe to the public to enlighten them in this matter, owing to the fact that there are now several manufacturers of chairs who have made and introduced in the market an imitation of our own styles of chairs, which they sell for Shakers' chairs, and which are unquestionably bought by the public generally under the impression that they are the real genuine article made by the Shakers at their establishment in Mount Lebanon, N.Y. Of all the imitations of our chairs which have come under our observation, there is none which we would be willing to accept as a specimen of our workmanship, nor would we be willing to stake our reputation on their merits.

There are a few House Furnishing and Furniture Dealers in some of the principal cities of the country to whom we sell our chairs, and some of those we have recently ascertained do keep and sell the imitation chairs, very much to our disgust and disapprobation; and all such we intend hereafter to discard and withdraw from them our trade, so that the public may be more secure in the purchase of the genuine article when purchasing of the dealers.

—An Illustrated Catalogue and Price List of the Shakers's Chairs, 1875

A number of chair companies contemporary to the Shakers attempted to capitalize upon the success and good name of the Shaker chair industry. Some of these companies openly sold their products as Shaker; they copied, sometimes closely, the design of the Shaker chair. Other companies advertised and sold their chairs as Shaker even though there were significant differences in style; some bore no resemblance at all.

One company that is representative of the *imitators* is the Enterprise Chair Mfg. Co. which operated in Oxford and Pitcher, New York, in the 1870s through the 1890s. Their 1887 and 1888 trade catalogues can be found in the Tannehill Library of the Edison Institute in Dearborn, Michigan. These catalogues have an accompanying price list which offers a #8 rocker for $9.25 (varnish) and a #11 *Gent's large* rocker for $32 (varnish) or $36 (ebony and gilt).

These chairs were advertised as Shaker despite obvious differences between the Enterprise and New Lebanon production chairs. Enterprise chairs have vertical spindles instead of back slats, posts mortised into rockers rather than rockers slotted into the posts, vase turnings that are gradually shaped rather than sharply defined, and no side seat stretchers. A.P. Hyde of the Enterprise firm patented a canvas seat which stretched between the front and back seat stretchers and was used on children's chairs and folding stools; a solid slip seat was used on adult chairs. An advertisement for a similar spindle back chair made by the Alfred E. Stacey Co. from Elbridge, New York, appeared in *The Furniture Worker* of August 10, 1890.

People who knew Sister Lillian Barlow and Brother William Perkins relate discussions with them in which they spoke of spindle back chairs. They repaired but did not manufacture them. Despite the fact that the Shakers did not make this style of chair, it continues to be thought of as Shaker.

Another company whose chairs have long been incorrectly called Shaker is The Henry I. Seymour Chair Manufactory of Troy, New York. An illustration in a ca. 1880 catalogue from the A.S. Herenden Furniture Co. in Cleveland, Ohio, offers an example of how this confusion may have begun. The Seymour chair is advertised as a *Shaker Rocker*.

While others used the Shaker name on their products, the Shakers did not sell chairs made by other manufacturers. They did, though, repair chairs made elsewhere. The 1884 chair order book records receiving *1 Seymour Chair for repairs* on November 14 and delivering it on the 26th. Another entry for November 29 of the same year notes *1 Seymour Rocker No. 3 Web. reweb & revarnish.* A letter written on *R.M. Wagan & Co.* letterhead and dated June 18, 1907, is addressed to Mrs. Andrew Thompson and reads as follows:

> *Yours to sister Clarisa Jacobs (deceased) received. The sketch of Swiss Bow Rocker is the Seymour Rocker made years ago but out of business. They are not made any more.*
>
> *We enclosed our Catalogue. We can furnish the braid for the rocker you have, if you can get the work done or we would do it and it would be just as good as a New Chair. Braid 4¢ per yard.*
>
> *We enclose samples.*

Patent information regarding both the taped back and seat and bentwood chair frames are illustrated in this appendix. These documents, the existence of numerous labeled Seymour chairs, and the easily identifiable designs clearly separate these chairs from Shaker chairs. One Seymour armless rocker very similar to its Shaker counterpart is a labeled child's rocker. The most notable difference between the Seymour and Shaker chairs is the bentwood rocker seen on most Seymour chairs. Shaker chairs do not use the continuous bentwood construction to form rockers, posts or arms. A paper label can occasionally be found on the rear stretchers of Seymour chairs.

An early twentieth century New York City newspaper advertisement led to the research of the L. & G. Stickley Company of Fayetteville, New York, and the records of its early years. Now in the collection of the Henry Ford Museum, these documents show an entire line of furniture in the Shaker style. A reference in *Furniture World* for May 16, 1918, relates the reorganization of the Stickley firm: *For the trade, the Stickleys are still building mission furniture, bedroom furniture, Shaker rockers.* David Cathers in his book, *Furniture Of The American Arts and Crafts Movement,* refers to the new company formed by four of the Stickley brothers at the time of the demise of the firm owned by Gustav Stickley: *The first ad for this new combination appeared . . . in 1918, showing . . . a new line, 'Berkshire,' based on Shaker furniture design.* The numbering of the style used in the catalogues confirms the 1918 date. For many years, this particular chair has been incorrectly called "Hancock Shaker."

Most of these chairs made by the Stickley Company, which is still in business, are easily distinguishable by their chestnut wood, the shape of the pommels, the ungainly bent back post, small mushroom tenon caps and unusual proportions creating a very deep seated chair. These chairs which were apparently not labeled can be accurately identified by comparison with the original advertisements illustrated here.

UNITED STATES PATENT OFFICE.

GROVE M. HARWOOD, OF TROY, AND ROBERT WOOD, OF WEST TROY, NEW YORK, ASSIGNORS TO "THE HENRY I. SEYMOUR CHAIR MANUFACTORY," OF SAME PLACE.

DESIGN FOR CHAIRS.

Specification forming part of Design No. 6,875, dated September 9, 1873; application filed July 26, 1873.
[Term of Patent 7 years.]

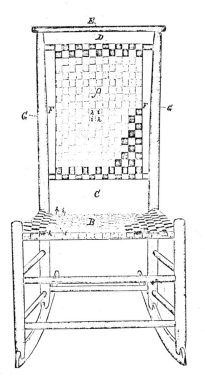

To all whom it may concern:

Be it known that we, GROVE M. HARWOOD, of Troy, in the county of Rensselaer and State of New York, and ROBERT WOOD, of West Troy, in the county of Albany and State aforesaid, have jointly invented and produced a new and original Design for Chairs, of which the following is a specification, reference being had, by letters, to the accompanying photograph of a chair which embodies the distinguishing features of our said design.

One part of our invention consists of the design for the back of a chair as distinguished by the checkered back-rest A, having light and dark or different-colored square or rectangular surfaces h and i arranged alternately with each other in both upright and horizontal rows, the back posts G G, with supports extending therefrom to the corners of the said back-rest, and the intervening open spaces F, F, and C, all shaped and arranged together so as to present an appearance substantially the same as is represented in the aforesaid photograph. Another part of our invention consists of the design for a chair as distinguished by the checkered seat B, having alternate light and dark or different-colored square or rectangular surfaces h and i arranged in rows crossing each other, the checkered back-rest A, the back posts G G, with supports ex-

tending therefrom to the corners of the said back-rest, and the inclosed vacant spaces C and F F, all shaped and arranged together so as to present substantially the same appearance as is shown in the photograph aforesaid.

In carrying out our aforesaid invention the backs of the chairs are to be manufactured with or without a top rail, E, and an inclosed vacant space, D, underneath.

What we claim as our invention is—

1. The design for the back of a chair as distinguished by the checkered back-rest A, back posts G G, with supports extending therefrom to the corners of the said back-rest, and intervening vacant spaces F, F, and C, all shaped and arranged together as herein described.

2. The design for a chair as distinguished by the checkered seat B, checkered back-rest A, back posts G G, with supports extending therefrom to the corners of the said back-rest, and inclined vacant spaces C and F F, all shaped and arranged together as described.

In testimony whereof we hereunto subscribe our names this 24th day of July, 1873.
GROVE M. HARWOOD.
ROBERT WOOD.

Witnesses:
GEORGE C. HASTINGS,
AUSTIN F. PARK.

The examples illustrated in the appendix offer an insight into the Shakers' need to warn their patrons about *the imitators*. With the advertising that existed, it is easy to see how the confused identity of many of these chairs continued.

The differences between the Shaker chairs and those of their contemporaries, competitors and imitators are often obvious even to the untrained eye. In other cases, however, a careful examination is required to detect the differences. The comparison of various components-pommels, posts, rockers, arms and the chair as a whole, with the chairs illustrated in this book should help to determine the identity of a given chair. Was it made by the Shakers or by the Imitators?

No. 90.

Shaker Bow Rocker, made of Bent Rock Elm, light or Ebony finish, handsomely upholstered in Worsted Tape, in all colors. Price $6.75.

We upholster also in Raw Silks, with Borders. Send for Photographs of two dozen other styles Shaker Chairs and Rockers.

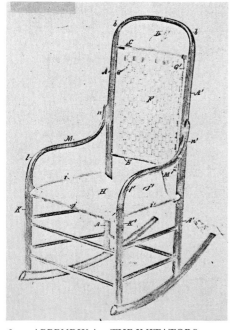

What we claim as our joint invention is—

1. The design for the back of a chair, composed of the round side posts A A', which extend below the seat and form the rear legs of the chair, and are tapered and curved inward at the upper parts *b b'*, and united in reduced diameter and bow form at the top, and the upper and lower cross-bars C and E, and intervening quadrilateral back-rest F, all shaped and arranged together, as specified and shown.

2. The design for the middle portion of the chair, composed of the seat H, with four sides, *i i' j j'*, the round rear posts A A' forming the rear legs and the side posts of the back, the upper and lower cross-bars C E, and intervening quadrilateral back-rest F, and the front posts K K', round in cross-section, and forming the front legs, and tapered and curved at *l l'* above the seat, and extended rearward in reduced diameter, and in the form of small round curved arm-rests M M', to and against the round rear posts, all shaped and arranged together, as shown and described.

3. The design for a chair, composed of the round rear posts A A', tapered, curved, and united together in bow form at the top, cross-bars C E, back-rest F, seat H, and round front posts K K', tapered, curved, and extended upward and rearward to and against the back posts, all substantially as represented in the aforesaid photograph.

In testimony whereof we hereunto subscribe our names this 12th day of October, 1874.

GROVE M. HARWOOD.
ROBERT WOOD.

Witnesses:
FRANK A. ANDROS,
GEORGE C. HASTINGS.

1-3 Illustrations from the catalogue of the E.H. Mahoney Company of Boston, Massachusetts, ca.1880. Shaker influenced chairs. (Reprinted from *Furniture, Made in America* by Richard and Eileen Dubrow, Published by Schiffer Publishing Ltd.)

4 Advertisements from "Furniture World," August 10, 1888. (Reprinted from *The Rocking Chair Book* by Ellen and Bert Denker)

1

2

3

Alfred E. Stacey,

MANUFACTURER OF

FANCY

ROCKERS

PLUSH,

LEATHER

AND

CARPET

COVERED.

Camp Stools and Folding Chairs.

SEND FOR PRICE LIST.

4 ELBRIDGE, N. Y.

Chairs from catalogue, ca.1885, of the Enterprise Chair Mfg. Co., Oxford, N.Y. Spindle backs, small mushroom tenon caps at handholds, mortising of posts into rockers, and the absence of side seat stretchers distinguish Enterprise chairs from those made by the Shakers. (Courtesy of Henry Ford Museum, The Edison Institute, Dearborn, Michigan)

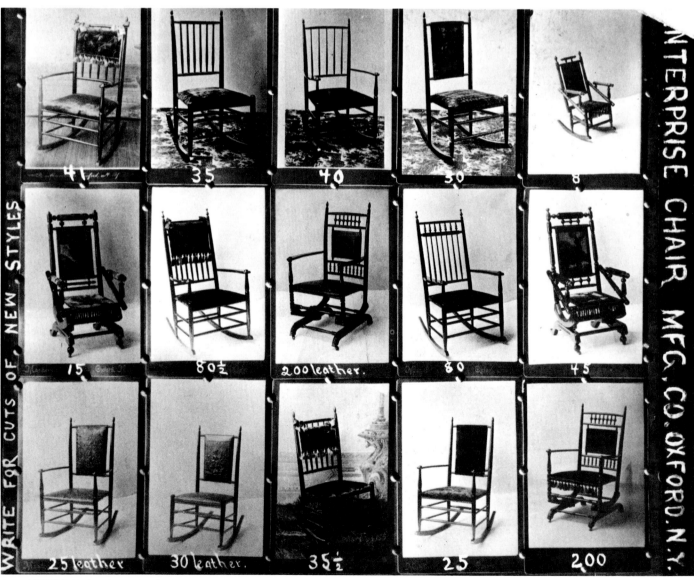

Advertisement from "American Agriculturist," 1888. The patent on this and other "Shaker" platform rockers was held by a W.I. Bunker of Chicago. One of the imitators' platform rockers utilizing this patented rocker mechanism is in the collection at Canterbury Shaker Village. The rocker frame above the seat is a close copy of the Shaker production armed rocker. However, neither the frame nor the rocker mechanism is Shaker made. (Courtesy of Hancock Shaker Village, Inc., Pittsfield, Massachusetts)

No. 297. Patent Shaker Rocker.

Given for a Club of 16 Subscribers at $1 each, or for 8 Subscribers and $2 Additional.

This is an elegant chair, and it merits attention not only for the low price and novelty, but for its good work, good finish and solid comfort. It is made of imitation mahogany, upholstered in velvet of a rich pattern, and finished with fringe. It has a heavily webbed seat and back, which are very strong and pliable, giving the body ease and grace. When shipped it is set up ready for use. For beauty, comfort and cheapness this is the perfection of chairs, and every house ought to contain one of these rockers.

Price $5. By express or freight at expense of receiver.

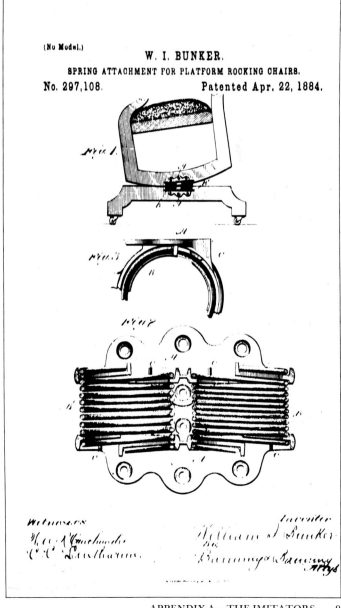

(No Model.)

W. I. BUNKER.
SPRING ATTACHMENT FOR PLATFORM ROCKING CHAIRS.
No. 297,108.   Patented Apr. 22, 1884.

200 Old-fashioned Shaker Chairs

Greatly Lowered for Speedy Clearaway

200 mahogany-finished Shaker chairs and rockers by Stickley of Fayetteville, known for years as a maker of fine furniture.

Restful and comfortable, these chairs are most desirable for sitting-rooms, bed-rooms, or in any spot where light, good-looking furniture is wanted.

Seats are upholstered in figured cretonnes of varied designs.

The exact quantities for tomorrow's selling

85 **Side chairs at $6 for $9 grade.**
55 **Side rockers at $6.75 for $10 grade.**
8 **Side chairs at $8.25 for the $12.50 grade.**
5 **Side rockers at $9 for the $13.50 grade.**
14 **Arm chairs at $11.75 for the $18 grade.**
13 **Arm rockers at $12.50 for the $18 grade.**
15 **Arm chairs at $14.50 for the $20.50 grade.**
6 **Arm rockers at $15 for the $21.50 grade.**

Fifth Gallery, New Building.

1

2

3

4

BIBLIOGRAPHY

PRINTED MATERIAL

Alexander, John D., Jr. MAKE A CHAIR FROM A TREE: AN INTRODUCTION TO WORKING GREEN WOOD. Newton, Connecticut: The Taunton Press, 19.

AN ILLUSTRATED CATALOGUE AND PRICE LIST OF THE SHAKERS' CHAIRS, FOOT BENCHES, FLOOR MATS, ETC. MANUFACTURED AND SOLD BY THE SHAKERS, AT MT. LEBANON, COLUMBIA CO., N.Y. Lebanon Springs, New York: B.F. Reynolds, Book, Card, and Job Printer, 1875.

Andrews, Edward Deming. THE COMMUNITY INDUSTRIES OF THE SHAKERS. Albany, New York: The University of the State of New York, 1933.

_____. THE PEOPLE CALLED SHAKERS. New York: Oxford University Press, 1953.

_____. RELIGION IN WOOD: A BOOK OF SHAKER FURNITURE. Bloomington, Indiana: Indiana University Press, 1966.

_____. SHAKER FURNITURE: THE CRAFTSMANSHIP OF AN AMERICAN COMMUNAL SECT. New Haven: Yale University Press, 1937.

Andrews, Edward Deming and Faith. VISIONS OF THE HEAVENLY SPHERE. Charlottesville: The University Press of Virginia. Published for The Henry Francis DuPont Winterthur Museum, 1969.

THE BERKSHIRE EVENING EAGLE. Pittsfield, Massachusetts: December 29, 1923.

_____. August 13, 1933.

Bishop, Robert. CENTURIES AND STYLES OF THE AMERICAN CHAIR 1640-1970. New York: E.P. Dutton & Co., Inc., 1972.

Blinn, Henry C. GENTLE MANNERS. East Canterbury, New Hampshire: The United Society, 1899.

CATALOGUE AND PRICE LIST OF SHAKERS' CHAIRS. Pittsfield, Massachusetts: Press of Geo. T. Denny, post-1876.

_____. (Canaan, N.Y.:) Canaan Printing Co.

Cathers, David. FURNITURE OF THE AMERICAN ARTS AND CRAFTS MOVEMENT. New York: New American Library, 1981.

CENTENNIAL ILLUSTRATED CATALOGUE AND PRICE LIST OF THE SHAKERS' CHAIRS, FOOT BENCHES, FLOOR MATS, ETC. MANUFACTURED AND SOLD BY THE SHAKERS, AT MT. LEBANON, COLUMBIA CO., N.Y. Albany: Weed, Parsons & Co., Printers. 1876.

Denker, Ellen and Bert. THE ROCKING CHAIR BOOK. New York: Mayflower Books, Inc., 1979.

Dubrow, Eileen and Richard. FURNITURE MADE IN AMERICA 1875-1905. Exton, Pennsylvania: Schiffer Publishing Ltd., 1982.

Elkins, Hervey. FIFTEEN YEARS IN THE SENIOR ORDER OF THE SHAKERS. Hanover, New Hampshire: Dartmouth Press, 1853.

Emlen, Robert. "The Best Shaker Chairs Ever Made," MAINE ANTIQUE DIGEST.

Filley, Dorothy M. Ed. by Mary L. Richmond. RECAPTURING WISDOM'S VALLEY: THE WATERVLIET SHAKER HERITAGE, 1775-1975. Published by the Town of Colonie and the Albany Institute of History and Art. New York: Publishing Center for Cultural Resources, 1975.

Frances, Evan. "American Classic, Furnishings in the Shaker Manner." FAMILY CIRCLE, June, 1964, pp. 42-46.

Handberg, Ejner. SHOP DRAWINGS OF SHAKER FURNITURE AND WOODENWARE, VOLUME I. Stockbridge, Massachusetts: The Berkshire Traveller Press, 1973.

_____. SHOP DRAWINGS OF SHAKER FURNITURE AND WOODENWARE, VOLUME II. Stockbridge, Massachusetts: The Berkshire Traveller Press, 1975.

Harrison, Barbara. "The Background of Shaker Furniture." NEW YORK HISTORY. Vol. 29, No. 3, July, 1948, pp. 319-326.

Hornung, Clarence P. TREASURY OF AMERICAN DESIGN: VOLUME TWO. New York: Harry N. Abrams, Inc.

Hults, Barbara Coeyman. "Shaker Chairs," AMERICAN ART AND ANTIQUES. November-December, 1978.

ILLUSTRATED CATALOGUE AND PRICE LIST OF THE SHAKERS' CHAIRS. New York: R.M. Wagan and Co., 1874.

_____. 1875.

Jackson, Paula Rice. "On Decorating and Design: The Silent Eloquence of Classic Shaker Chairs," HOUSE BEAUTIFUL, November, 1982.

Johnson, Theodore E. and John McKee. HANDS TO WORK AND HEARTS TO GOD: THE SHAKER TRADITION IN MAINE. Brunswick: Bowdoin College Museum of Art, 1969.

Kassay, John. THE BOOK OF SHAKER FURNITURE. Amherst: The University of Massachusetts Press, 1980.

Klamkin, Marian. HANDS TO WORK: SHAKER FOLK ART AND INDUSTRIES. New York: Dodd, Mead & Company, 1972.

Kovel, Ralph and Terry. AMERICAN COUNTRY FURNITURE, 1789-1875. New York: Crown Publishers, Inc., 1965.

Lassiter, William L. "Shakers and Their Furniture." NEW YORK HISTORY. Vol. 27, July, 1946, pp. 369-371.

MacLean, J.P. SHAKERS OF OHIO. Columbus, Ohio: Ohio Historical and Archaelogical Society, 1907.

THE MANIFESTO, Shaker Village, New Hampshire: July, 1895.

_____. November, 1889.

MARSHALL FIELD & COMPANY: CHAIRS AND ROCKERS MANUFACTURED BY THE SOCIETY OF SHAKERS AT MOUNT LEBANON, N.Y. Chicago: Marshall Field & Co., circa 1900.

Meader, Robert F.W. ILLUSTRATED GUIDE TO SHAKER FURNITURE. New York: Dover Publications, Inc., 1972.

Melcher, Marguerite F. "Shaker Furniture." PHILADELPHIA MUSEUM BULLETIN. Vol. LXII, Spring, 1962, pp. 89-92.

Morse, Flo. THE SHAKERS AND THE WORLD'S PEOPLE. New York: Dodd, Mead & Company, 1980.

Muller, Charles. "It Looks Shaker, It's Called Shaker, But It's Stickley." OHIO ANTIQUE REVIEW, Vol. 8, April, 1982, p. 8-10.

_____. THE SHAKER WAY. Worthington, Ohio: Ohio Antique Review, 1979.

_____. "They Look Like Shaker, But..." OHIO ANTIQUE REVIEW, Vol. 8, March, 1982, p. NS 6-7.

Ott, John Harlow. HANCOCK VILLAGE: A GUIDEBOOK AND HISTORY. Hancock, Massachusetts: Shaker Community, Inc., 1976.

Pearson, Elmer R. and Julia Neal. THE SHAKER IMAGE. Boston: New York Graphic Society in collaboration with Shaker Community, Inc., 1974.

THE PEG BOARD: FIRST SHAKER NUMBER. June, 1936. Lebanon School, New Lebanon, New York (Reprint), Darrow School, 1966.

Peladeau, Marius B. "Early Shaker Chairs," HISTORIC PRESERVATION. Vol. 22, No. 4, October-December, 1970.

Phillips, Hazel Spencer. RICHARD THE SHAKER. Oxford, Ohio: Typoprint Inc., 1972.

Piercy, Caroline B. THE VALLEY OF GOD'S PLEASURE: A SAGA OF THE NORTH UNION SHAKER COMMUNITY. New York: Stratford House, 1951.

PRICE LIST OF SHAKERS CHAIRS. MANUFACTURED IN THE UNITED SOCIETY, NEW LEBANON, COLUMBIA CO., N.Y.

Ray, Mary Lyn. "A Reappraisal of Shaker Furniture and Society," WINTERTHUR PORTFOLIO 8, Edited by Ian M.G. Quimby. Charlottesville: The University Press of Virginia, Published for The Henry Francis DuPont Winterthur Museum, 1973.

———. Introduction, TRUE GOSPEL SIMPLICITY: SHAKER FURNITURE IN NEW HAMPSHIRE. Concord. The New Hampshire Historical Society, 1974.

Rhodus, Jack. "Ohio Shaker Chairs," THE SHAKER MESSENGER, Vol. 5, No. 2, Winter, 1983, p. 12.

Richmond, Mary L., compiler and annotator. SHAKER LITERATURE: A BIBLIOGRAPHY, IN TWO VOLUMES. Hanover, New Hampshire: Shaker Community, Inc., 1977.

Santore, Charles. THE WINDSOR STYLE IN AMERICA. Philadelphia: Running Deer Press, 1981.

THE SHAKER. Watervliet, New York, September, 1872.

THE SHAKER HERITAGE. Shaker Heights: The Shaker Historical Society, 1980.

A SHAKER READER, Edited by Milton C. and Emily Mason Rose. New York: Universe Press, 1975.

THE SHAKERS: AN EXHIBITION CONCERNING THEIR FURNITURE, ARTIFACTS, AND RELIGION WITH EMPHASIS ON ENFIELD, CONNECTICUT. Hartford: The Women's Auxiliary of the United Cerebral Palsy Association of Greater Hartford, 1975.

THE SHAKERS: PURE OF SPIRIT, PURE OF MIND. Duxbury, Massachusetts: Art Complex Museum, 1983.

Shea, John G. THE AMERICAN SHAKERS AND THEIR FURNITURE. New York: Van Nostrand, 1971.

Sprigg, June. BY SHAKER HANDS. New York: Alfred A. Knopf, 1975.

SPRINGFIELD REPUBLICAN. Springfield, Massachusetts: December 29, 1923.

Stearns, Ezra. HISTORY OF ASHBURNHAM. Rindge, New Hampshire: 1887.

Williams, Roger M. "Shaker of the West," AMERICANA, Vol. 7, No. 1, March-April, 1979.

MANUSCRIPTS

Albany, New York. New York State Library, Manuscripts Division. "Census of Manufacturers in Columbia County, New York," 1850, 1860, 1880.

———. "Hancock Record Book, 1789-1801."

———. "Memoranda, &¢. Mostly of Events and Things which have transpired since the first of Jan. 1846.," (Thomas Damon).

Bowling Green, Kentucky. Kentucky Library, Western Kentucky University. Typescript of "Journal A," Kept at South Shakertown at South Union.

———. Typescript of "Journal B," Volumes 1 and 2, 1837-1864, Kept at South Union.

Canterbury, New Hampshire. Shaker Village. "Historical Record of Church Family, 1890-1930."

———. "Diary of Henry Blinn," 1872.

Charlestown, Massachusetts. Collection of Cynthia Elyce Rubin. Letter to Mrs. Andrew Thompson from R.M. Wagan & Co.

Chicago. Pearson Collection. "Checks written on the Agricultural National Bank of Pittsfield by The R.M. Wagan & Co." 1884-1921.

Cleveland, Ohio. Western Reserve Historical Society. Shaker Collection II-B-38. "Inventory of the money and stock held at the beginning of each year," 1839-1864, New Lebanon.

———. II-B-45. "Account book of sales and purchases," 1844-1866, North Union.

———. V-B-68. A domestic journal of domestic occurances, 1834-1846, New Lebanon.

———. II-B-83. "Account Book-Feb. 7, 1844-April 18, 1860," South Union.

———. IV-A-10. White, Jefferson. Letter to "Elder Grove," from Enfield, Connecticut.

———. IV-A-12. ———, Betty. Letter to "Br. Daniel Hawkins," February 21, 1834.

———. IV-A-13. Letter to "Dearly beloved & much esteemed ministry," from Enfield, New Hampshire, May 5, 1841.

———. IV-A-14. ———, Grove. Letter from City of Union, August 31, 1853.

———. IV-A-20. Letter to "Beloved Elder Grove" from West Pittsfield, December 2, 1853.

———. IV-A-26. Letter "Kind & dearest friend, Elder Grove."

———. IV-A-26. Letter to "Brother Elder Grove" from Watch-Hill, August 25, 1853.

———. V-B-68. "A domestic journal of domestic occurences at Mount Lebanon, New York," 1814-1833.

———. V-B-71. "A domestic journal of domestic occurences," 1856-1877, New Lebanon.

———. V-B-118. "Journals and diaries kept by Giles B. Avery," 1872, New Lebanon.

———. V-B-167. "Journal of the South Family, 1874-1878," New Lebanon.

———. V-B-168. "Journal of the South Family, 1878-1883," New Lebanon.

———. V-B-218. "Journal of the activities of the ministry at both Shirley and Harvard."

———. V-B-279 through 282. "Records of the Church at Watervliet, New York," 1788-1851.

———. V-B-285 through 296. Wells, Freegift. "Memorandum of Events," 1812-1865.

———. V-B-315. "The Record and Journal of the Sisters written in the First Order at Watervliet," 1830-1841.

———. 015278. "Wagan, Robert M."

Columbus, Ohio. Ohio Historical Society. Shaker Collection. "Account Book," October 16, 1856-September 1, 1872, Watervliet, Ohio.

———. Box 7. Prescott, James. "Diary of James Prescott, 1860."

Enfield, New Hampshire. Private Collection. "A Historical Narrative of the Rise and Progress of the United Society of Shakers, Enfield, N.H., 1858."

———. "Historical Notes Having Reference to the Believers in Enfield, N.H. by Henry C. Blinn," 1897. Two Volumes.

Harrodsburg, Kentucky. Mercer County Historical Society. "A Journal kept by Polly Harris for the benefit of the sisters at the West Family containing all the important moves and changes and when they began. January 1, 1858-1867."

Harvard, Massachusetts. Fruitlands Museums. "A Journal containing some of the most important events of the day kept for use & convenience of the Brethren of the church."

_____. "Financial Account, 1825-1836."

Lexington, Kentucky. King Library, University of Kentucky. Shakertown at Pleasant Hill Manuscript Collection. "Pleasant Hill, Account Book, 1815-1817—Thomas Logan."

Louisville, Kentucky. The Filson club. BA S-526. "Account Book, 1842-1849," Pleasant Hill.

_____. BA S-527. "Deaconesses' Domestic Concerns, 1843-1871," Pleasant Hill.

_____. BA S-527. "A Temporal Journal Kept by order of the Deacons of the East House . . . Book B," Pleasant Hill.

_____. Unpublished manuscript by Max Charleston entitled "The Shakers of Kentucky."

New York. The New York Public Library. Shaker Manuscripts.

Old Chatham, New York. Shaker Museum Emma King Library. "Journey to Kentucky" by Elder H.C. Blinn, 1873.

_____. Yearly Inventories for 1853, 1854, 1860.

Pittsfield, Massachusetts. Berkshire Athenaeum. Letter to H.H. Ballard from William Perkins, October 21, 1924.

_____. Hancock Shaker Village, Inc. No. 381. Account book, 1875.

_____. No. 389. Account book, 1876.

_____. No. 54. Account book, 1877.

_____. Collins, Sarah. Letter of October 3, 1924.

Sabbathday Lake, Maine. United Society of Shakers. "Alfred, Maine, Book # 2," January 10, 1806-1809.

_____. "No. 1 Ledger Book, 1804, Alfred."

Washington, D.C., Library of Congress. Shaker Collection Item No. 2. "Family Expenses paid by Martha Pease and Anna in the year 1865."

_____. Item No. 43. Lyon, Benjamin. "Journal of Benjamin Lyon of Canaan, June 12, 1816-Feb. 8, 1818, concerning events in the family of the second order."

_____. Item No. 45. Lyon, Benjamin. "A Journal of Work," 1834-1838, New Lebanon.

_____. Item No. 152. "Financial Account of the Shaker Community in the Miami Valley, Ohio," 1807-1815.

_____. Item No. 252. "Summary of notes on events at Union Village," 1805-1843.

_____. Item No. 347b. McNemar, Richard R. Letter to "Much Esteemed Br. Rufus," October 28, 1837.

_____. National Gallery of Art. Index of American Design.

Winterthur, Delaware. The Henry Francis DuPont Winterthur Museum. Edward Deming Andrews Memorial Shaker Collection. SA 813. "Memmo of Movebel Estate of Gideon Turner," 1788.

_____. SA 894. "Journal Kept by the Deaconesses at the office. Work done by the Sisters in the year," 1841-1869, New Lebanon.

_____. SA 904. Account Book, "Order book-Chair Room, New Lebanon, N.Y.," 1874-1875.

_____. SA 904. "Notice to our Patrons, R.M. Wagan & Co. Mt. Lebanon, N.Y. 1874."

_____. SA 904.3. Letter to "Dear Sister Anna."

_____. SA 905. Account Book, "Order book-Chair Room, New Lebanon, N.Y.," 1884-1885.

_____. SA 934. "Receipt book, R.M. Wagan & Co. Mount Lebanon," 1884-1895.

_____. SA 1000.1. "Number of Chairs left at the Second Family."

_____. SA 1031. Lyon, Benjamin. "Journal of Domestic Events including 1840," New Lebanon.

_____. SA 1409.8. Hall, Frances. Letter to Margaret Brown, New Lebanon, New York, 1944.

_____. SA 1447. Advertisement from newspaper, "200 Old fashioned Shaker Chairs."

_____. SA 1685. Price List, "Shaker chairs manufactured by the Society of Shakers, Mt. Lebanon."

INDEX

THE SHAKER CHAIR
CHARLES R. MULLER   TIMOTHY D. RIEMAN

DRAWINGS BY STEPHEN METZGER

WATERVLIET
NEW YORK

ENFIELD
NEW HAMPSHIRE

CANTERBURY
NEW HAMPSHIRE

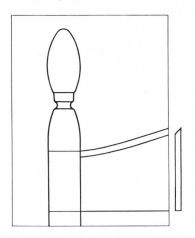

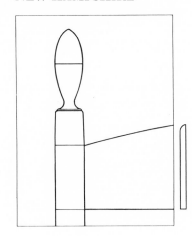

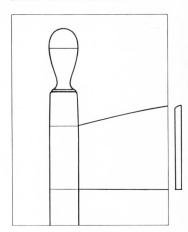

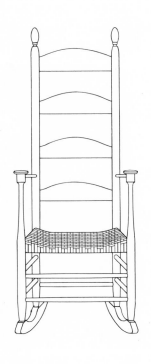

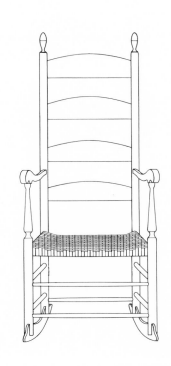

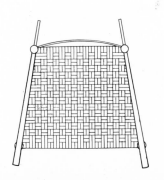

THE UNIVERSITY OF MASSACHUSETTS PRESS
Amherst

**TRANSITIONAL
MT. LEBANON
NEW YORK** ca. 1870

**R.M. WAGAN
MT. LEBANON
NEW YORK** post-1876

**PERKINS-BARLOW
MT. LEBANON
NEW YORK** ca. 1930

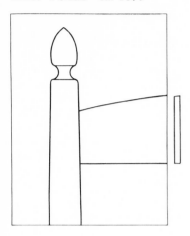

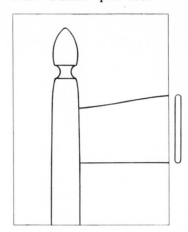

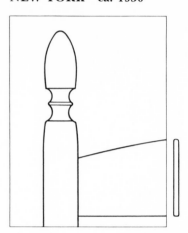

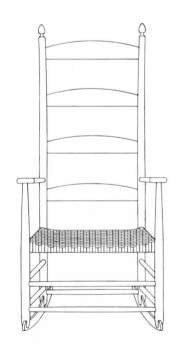

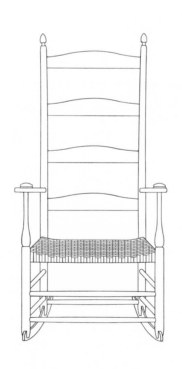

Elongated acorn-shaped pommels have their necks adorned with an added ring turning that is not seen on earlier chairs. On five slat examples, these have been turned separately and applied to the straight dowel stock used for posts. There is no bend, nor taper, although a minimal turning appears at the bottom of the posts. Slats have a continuous, sweeping arch. Front posts have vase turning between seat and arms. Arms are uniformly thick and have no projections at the wrists and elbows. Tenon caps are flatter and broader than earlier examples and usually extend beyond width of arms. Stretchers are purchased dowel stock and are of uniform diameter throughout their length. Rockers with curved front and backs are fastened with screws.

Acorn-shaped pommels are formed by turning a simple collar and a point on the top of the posts. A pronounced bend in the posts begins just above the seat and continues to a lesser degree to the top. Slats, rounded on the tops, are arched in the center and curve to be almost horizontal as they enter the posts. The front posts possess a vase turning between the seat and the arms. Uniformly thick, the broad, flat arms have projections at the wrist and elbow positions and have been rounded on the inside and outside edges by a shaper. The handholds are mushroom-shaped tenon caps. Stretchers are tapered. Rockers, terminating in curves on the front and back, are fastened to the posts with flathead screws.

Simply and uniformly turned pommels top gently tapered and bent back posts. There are no scribe marks indicating the placement of the gracefully arched slats. Top edges of the slats are slightly beveled. Front posts are tapered without embellishment from the seat to the arms. The side scroll arms, tapering in thickness from the front to the back, are rounded on the inside and beveled on the outside. Stretchers are tapered. Rockers are rounded on the front and possess a continuous arc between the posts which is duplicated at the back before turning downward to meet the underside of the blades. These are fastened to the posts with wood pins.

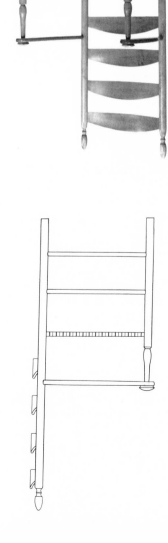

Rounded tops of pommels terminate in slight point and are divided from elongated lower section by scribe marks. Posts taper slightly from seat to top. Back slats, usually graduated, have strong arch and rounded bevel on top edges. Front posts have gently shaped vase turning before forming collar to meet blocked section of front scrolled arms. Curvature on top edges of rockers as well as the convex/concave fronts and ends are not as great as those on Enfield, N.H., chairs. Rockers do have a well-defined segment that turns upward where fitted into the posts.

Some chairs have pommels terminating in small dome shape turning and slats with convex shape on lower edges.

Elongated elliptical pommels terminating in a sharp point possess medial scribe marks. Smooth and graceful neck ends in small ridge leading to the finely rounded shoulders. Graduated wide and strongly arched slats, with top one pinned into posts from back, have rounded top edges. Slender front posts have vase turning before forming collar. Arms have front scrolled handholds that curve underneath before terminating in block for receiving tenon of posts. Arms narrow in width from front to mortise joint at back. Rockers begin and end in concave/convex shape and have sweeping curve across top between posts. On tilters, balls are half sphere and secured with leather thongs. Seat stretchers, often drilled for cane, occasionally held at posts with brads.

Elliptically shaped pommels have slightly rounded tops and collar on lower ends. Diameter of posts noticeably increases from well-defined shoulder to scribe mark for top slat. Straight posts terminate in gentle convex taper. Graduated back slats boldly arched and heavily chamfered on top front edges. Front posts possess continual reduction in diameter above seat before enlarging to collar for receiving tenon of crescent shaped arms. Enlarged tops of front posts form handholds.

Single slat, low back, chairs often lack pommels and terminate in minute dome-shaped turnings at the top of the posts.

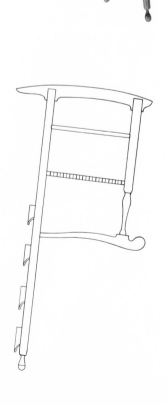

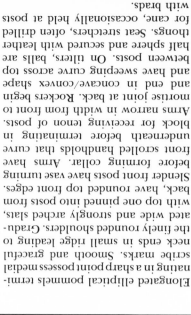

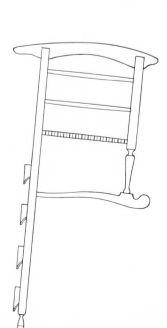

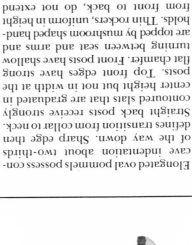

Bulbous pommels are adorned with double or triple scribe marks symmetrically around the midpoint. A small ridge defines the transition point from the neck to the shoulder of the back posts. The posts are abruptly bent just above the seat. The top one of the graduated slats is secured in the posts by single or double pins extending through the posts. Second slat from top is sometimes pinned. Stretchers taper to central scribe mark. Simple "bamboo" turning imitating. Front posts turned to slender diameter between seat and arms. Arms may be variation of drop scroll or side scroll, often with strong chamfer on underside. Rockers are simple in form and vary from ones of uniform width over their length to others with a straight top edge and much broader at the center than near the ends.

Elongated oval pommels possess concave indentation about two-thirds of the way down. Sharp edge then defines transition from collar to neck. Straight back posts receive strongly contoured slats that are graduated in center height but not in width at the posts. Top front edges have strong flat chamfer. Front posts have shallow turning between seat and arms and are topped by mushroom shaped handholds. Thin rockers, uniform in height from front to back, do not extend beyond front posts.

Some children's chairs have greatly elongated pommels and slats without the strong contour and heavy chamfer.

Well-turned, elongated pommels with single central scribe marks continue in an unbroken curve from the pointed tops to sharp shoulders. Single scribe marks on the back posts indicate the placement of slats and the depth of the rockers. Broad back slats, often graduated, possess a rounded bevel on the top front edges. Sometimes only the top slat is beveled. Front posts are gently tapered between seat and arms. Front scrolled arms are heavily chamfered on the underside of the handholds. Rockers usually have a continuous arc on the top from the curved front to the curved back and are fastened to the posts by rivets and burrs.

On tilters, balls are half sphere and fastened with leather thongs secured with tacks at level of lowest stretcher.

Oval shaped pommels, flattened on the top, possess a noticeable ridge before descending to the small neck and shoulder of the straight back posts. The posts, about one inch from the bottom, are sharply concave tapered. Back slats are arched on top edges and gently concaved on lower ones. Use of hand tools in chamfering of curvature is apparent. Mustard yellow is dominant color.

Bulbous pommels with elongated necks extend to rounded shoulders atop the straight back posts. Deeply bent graduated slats have strong contour that flows to nearly horizontal line before entering the slightly tapered posts. Front posts have a symmetrical turning adorned by concentric scribe marks between the seat and the arms. A variation of the side scroll arm extends beyond the support and is capped with a rounded handhold secured to the arm with pins or screws. Crescent shaped rockers extend beyond the posts.

Extremely delicate side chairs possess elongated oval pommels, and curved slats rounded on the front top edges. Seat stretchers are often pinned to posts.

Finely turned elliptical pommels are used on chairs having strongly arched back slats with rounded front edges. These are fastened into the posts with pins from the back. On side chairs, posts are tapered over their length and terminate in concave turning. On rockers, posts often terminate in swell turning or "boot." Front posts possess vase turning between seat and arms and usually support distinctive S-curve arms, uniform in thickness. Rockers have scrolled front edges. Orange is dominant color.

A variation of the Ohio chair lacks pommels and is distinguished by its chamfered back posts and corner-notched slats, often graduated in width and secured with brads from the front.

**NORTH UNION
UNION VILLAGE
WATERVLIET
WHITEWATER, OHIO**

**PLEASANT HILL
KENTUCKY**

**SOUTH UNION
KENTUCKY**

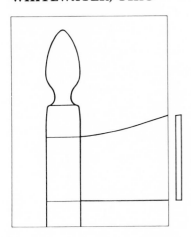

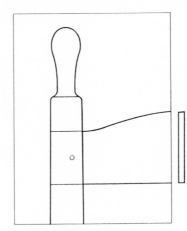

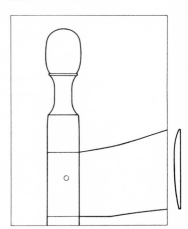

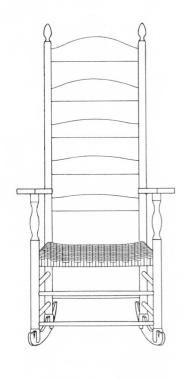

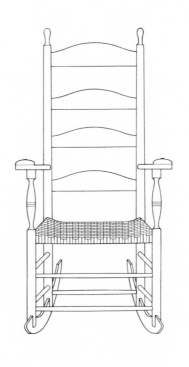

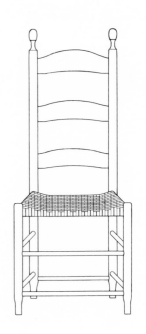

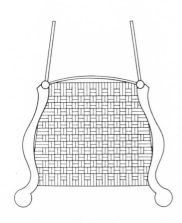

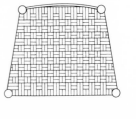

HARVARD
MASSACHUSETTS

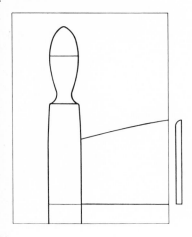

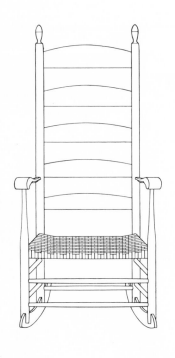

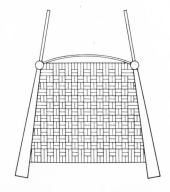

ENFIELD
CONNECTICUT

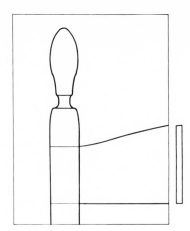

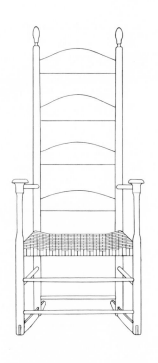

ALFRED
SABBATHDAY LAKE
MAINE

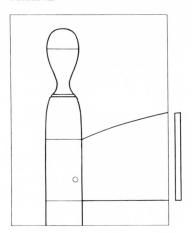

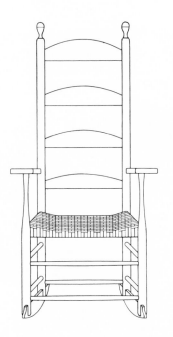

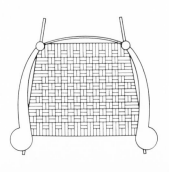